OSPREY AIRCRAFT OF THE ACES® • 53

Fokker D VII Aces
of World War 1
Part 1

SERIES EDITOR: TONY HOLMES

OSPREY AIRCRAFT OF THE ACES® • 53

Fokker D VII Aces of World War 1
Part 1

Norman Franks and Greg VanWyngarden

OSPREY
PUBLISHING

Front cover
On 6 June 1918, 19-year-old Ltn
Georg von Hantelmann of *Jasta* 15,
Jagdgeschwader II, achieved his
first victory. He was probably flying
Fokker D VII 382/18, decorated with
his grim personal insignia which
was based on the badge of his
former unit, the *Braunschweiger*
'death's head' Hussar Regiment
Nr 17. Under the leadership of the
seasoned *Jagdstaffel* commander
Joseph 'Seppl' Veltjens, the *Staffel's*
Fokkers intercepted a flight of seven
DH 4 bombers near Chaulnes – these
aircraft were probably from the
newly-formed Royal Air Force's
No 27 Sqn. Von Hantelmann's
fellow *Jasta* 15 pilot Joachim von
Ziegesar wrote a lively account of
this event several years later, in
which he erred in recalling their
opponents as 'French' aircraft;

'We are dressed and sitting in our
machines. Before every flight the
engine is first "braked" – a hellish
noise – then the machines are
rolling for take-off. Veltjens, as
leader, raises his hand and the wild
chase is on. While we climb with full
running engines, "Seppl" leads us to
the front so that we cut off the
enemy's way back. Soon we are at
4000 metres, then we catch sight of
them. Veltjens gives us the signal to
attack! Like a steer unbound, the
aircraft with the Braunschweig
Hussar's crest dives into the enemy
first. Even before we others have a
chance to shoot, Hantelmann goes
down with his left wingman on the
Frenchmen (sic) flying in arrow
formation. Each one grabs hold of
his opponent and, as is normal in air
fighting, only a few minutes pass by
and the French (sic) squadron that
was in the process of returning
home no longer exists! Radiating
joy, we gather together again
around our leader and try, flushed
with victory, to find new battles. We
have hardly climbed out of our
machines when the usual dispute
arises. It is determined, though, that
Hantelmann was the first to bag an
opponent.'

Contrary to von Ziegesar's
exaggerated claim, the flight from
No 27 Sqn was not wiped out, but
they did lose DH 4 B2080, with Lts
M F Cunningham and W J Stockins
killed. Two more DH 4s from the
same flight were badly shot up but
returned with wounded observers.

First published in Great Britain in 2003 by Osprey Publishing,
Midland House, West Way, Botley, Oxford OX2 0PH, UK
443 Park Avenue South, New York, NY 10016, USA
www.ospreypublishing.com
© 2003 Osprey Publishing Limited

ISBN 1 84176 533 3
A CIP catalogue record for this book is available from the British Library
Edited by Tony Holmes
Page design by Tony Truscott
Cover Artwork by Iain Wyllie
Aircraft Profiles by Harry Dempsey
Scale Drawings by Mark Styling
Index by Alan Thatcher
Origination by Grasmere Digital Imaging, Leeds, UK
Printed in Hong Kong through Bookbuilders

05 06 07 08   10 9 8 7 6 5 4 3

EDITOR'S NOTE
To make this best-selling series as authoritative as possible, the Editor would be
interested in hearing from any individual who may have relevant photographs,
documentation or first-hand experiences relating to the world's elite pilots, and
their aircraft, of the various theatres of war. Any material used will be credited
to its original source. Please write to Tony Holmes at 16 Sandilands,
Chipstead, Sevenoaks, Kent, TN13 2SP Great Britain, or by e-mail at:
tony.holmes@osprey-jets.freeserve.co.uk

ACKNOWLEDGEMENTS
The authors wish to thank Rick Duiven, Peter Kilduff, Peter M Grosz, George
H Williams, Dr Volker Koos, H H Wynne, Dr Glen K Merrill, D S Abbott,
Ray Rimell, Colin Owers, Dave Roberts, Joern Leckschied, Volker Haeusler,
Dave Watts, the late Neal W O'Connor and so many others who supplied
photographs and data which helped in the compilation of this work. The superb
research and works of Alex Imrie were of particular use. Dr Larry Sall, Carole
Thomas and the rest of the staff of the History of Aviation Collection,
University of Texas, Dallas, were always helpful and patient during the authors'
research there. Finally, the authors are indebted to O'Brien Browne and Jan
Hayzlett for their generosity in supplying translations of German literature.

Both von Ziegesar and von
Hantelmann received credit for their
first victories that day, and the
young ex-hussar would claim
24 more kills before war's end,
including two American aces and
one French ace. Von Hantelmann
and his comrades from JG II were
among the most deadly exponents
of one of the Great War's best
fighters, the legendary Fokker D VII
(*Cover artwork by Iain Wyllie*)

CONTENTS

CHAPTER ONE

THE BEST FIGHTER FOR JG I 6

CHAPTER TWO

**JG II – BERTHOLD'S
BLUE BIRDS 50**

CHAPTER THREE

**LOERZER'S JG III –
AND THE BAVARIANS 72**

APPENDICES 89
COLOUR PLATES COMMENTARY 91
INDEX 96

THE BEST FIGHTER FOR JG I

Throughout 1917 and into the spring of 1918, the German *Jagdstaffel* pilots had fought a valiant air campaign against the British and French air arms on the Western Front. Their tactics, while basically defensive in nature, had nevertheless inflicted significant losses on the two Allied forces.

In contrast to this defensive approach, the British in particular had waged a forceful air offensive, continually taking the war to the enemy across the trench lines. The airmen of the Royal Flying Corps (RFC) had found to their cost just how good the German fighter pilots could be. Almost daily RFC and French aircraft flew into German-held territory on bombing and reconnaissance missions, supported by fighter patrols whose pilots sought out the *Jasta* pilots in order to protect the two-seaters.

Those German pilots had been a formidable foe to the British and French in early 1917, with 'Bloody April' still a festering memory. That month both Allied air forces had taken a beating with the arrival of the Albatros D III fighter. As the year progressed, the Albatros D V, D Va and Pfalz D III arrived as replacements, but these types proved disappointing. Furthermore, *Jagdstaffel* operations were continually hampered by a poor supply of both pilots and aircraft. The arrival in France of such superior Allied types as the SE 5a, Sopwith Triplane and Camel, Bristol F 2B, the

An inauspicious start for the Fokker D VII at *Jasta* 10. Ltn 'Fritz' Friedrichs unfortunately ran beyond the landing field in D VII 234/18 and into two parked Fokkers and aircraft tents. This is one of the few photos of an operational D VII which still bore iron cross markings on its upper wing. The crosses on the fuselage and tail have been altered to a thick *Balkenkreuz* form as ordered on 17 March 1918, in the style favoured by *Jasta* 10. The insignia were converted by using the widest portion of the iron cross arms as the bar width. This machine seems to have borne a white vertical band ahead of the fuselage cross, painted on the streaky camouflaged fuselage. The wings were covered in printed 'lozenge' fabric *(via VanWyngarden)*

French SPAD VII and later SPAD XIII tipped the scales in favour of the Allies, and the German fighter force fell into hard times.

The battle for air supremacy over the trenches was paramount to both sides so that their armies could launch assaults with support from the air. Virtually all these land battles became abject failures, with each side trying to punch a hole through the trench systems. The cost of a few yards often amounted to thousands of lives amongst the soldiers of both sides.

The biggest gain by either side came in March 1918 with the German assault Operation *Michael*, which managed to thrust deep into Allied lines. Particular inroads were made against the British Fifth Army on the Somme Front, from Arras in the north to Noyon in the south, the Germans pushing beyond Montdidier and Albert before running out of steam. In early April 1918 another push further north from Armentières broke through along a front held by the British First and Second Armies.

Above these titanic battles buzzed the fighters of the German Air Service, but they were still the Albatros and Pfalz types of 1917, along with the fewer, but still potent, Fokker Dr I triplanes. Despite a massive build-up of Allied machines, the German fighter pilots were still able to shoot down aircraft (including many from the newly-formed RAF) in goodly numbers. However, the German pilots knew full well that their machines were increasingly outmatched by the latest Allied fighters.

America had now also entered the fray, and although it had no aircraft of its own, there was no shortage of US aviators already in France, with many more about to arrive. The German assault had been timed to try and finally smash the deadlock which had characterised the Western Front since early 1915, knowing that the might of the Allies would only increase with the addition of US forces. Once this assault started to falter during April, the way to ultimate victory lay in doubt.

In the meantime, German fighter pilots had heard rumours of a new aeroplane – one which many of the top aces were talking about. Several had seen and test flown this latest fighter, and it augured well for the future. It might even help regain aerial supremacy. The new fighter was the Fokker D VII biplane, the latest from Anthony Fokker's stable. The first German fighter pilots of 1915-16 had achieved much with the Fokker Eindecker models. Despite these early aeroplanes being of indifferent quality, they were armed with a machine gun firing through the propeller, and flown by men determined to make a name for themselves, the Fokker monoplanes had achieved much in victories and reputation.

The next successful Fokker machine was the Dr I triplane, made famous by von Richthofen himself. Despite some early structural problems which resulted in the type being withdrawn from service for a short period, it became a successful fighter for a while, and is probably remembered and referred to more than any other aircraft of World War 1.

Yet even Manfred von Richthofen was fully aware that the life of the Dr I was limited, and a new machine was desperately needed. He too had been among the aces who had tested the new Fokker biplane prototype, and was eager to see its arrival at the front. In mid January 1918, new examples of fighter designs had been brought together at Adlershof, near Berlin, so that combat pilots could fly and evaluate them. The aircraft manufacturers, including Fokker, had been given the task of designing a new fighter around the existing 160-hp Mercedes D III in-line engine.

Von Richthofen was a great influence on all fighter matters, and he had helped to instigate these evaluations by frontline pilots. The meeting at Adlershof took place on 19 January, and he went along with one of his *Jasta* 11 pilots, Ltn Georg von der Osten. In all, there were 28 varying types tested. Fokker brought six rotary-engined designs and two Mercedes-engined fighters – the modified V 11 (w/n 1883) and the larger, heavier V 18 (w/n 2116). Of all the machines they saw, the Fokker V 11 was the one which caught the attention of most of the pilots.

One of the main features of the Fokker V 11 was its thick cantilever wings. Although initially the V 11 had some directional instability, by the time it had evolved into the Fokker D VII, this and other problems had been resolved. An initial order for 300 D VIIs was placed with the Fokker firm. Not only did the Fokker factory at Schwerin go into full production, but also the Albatros Factory at Johannisthal, and its subsidiary the Ostdeutsche Albatros Werke at Schneidemühl, were also ordered to produce 600 machines under licence. Johannisthal-built machines were designated D VII (Alb) and those from the Schneidemühl factory were D VII (OAW). The hard-pressed pilots of the *Jagdstaffeln* would finally have an aircraft which would prove a match for any opposing machine. Indeed, many German airmen considered the D VII the best all-around fighter of the entire war, a sentiment today echoed by many historians.

It was now just a matter of time before production D VIIs reached the front. For von Richthofen, now back in combat and still flying the rotary-engined Dr I, they would not arrive in time. Operation *Michael* had commenced and the Rittmeister had brought his score to an astounding 80 by 20 April. Keen to add more before another leave came, he chased a Camel a little too far on the 21st, misjudged the wind direction and found himself over Allied territory at low level. Hit by a single bullet fired from the ground, von Richthofen died as he crash landed.

He had been harassing the high command since March for the D VII. Indeed, on 2 April 1918 he had written to an old friend, Oblt Fritz von Falkenhayn, technical officer at the *Kogenluft* (*Kommandierenden General der Luftstreitkräfte* – General in command of the German Army Air Service) office in Berlin, asking;

'After a long time I come once again with a question. When can I count on the arrival of Fokker biplanes and with the super-compressed engines?

'The superiority of British single-seat and reconnaissance aircraft makes it even more perceptibly unpleasant here. The single-seaters fight coming over at high altitude and stay there. One cannot even shoot at them. Speed is the most important point. One could shoot down five to ten times as many if we were faster. During the offensive we liked the low cloud ceiling, because at low altitude the triplane has its advantages. Please give me news soon about when we can count on these new machines.'

THE FOKKER D VII ARRIVES

In this first volume on D VII aces, we will cover the *Jagdstaffeln* of the four army *Jagdgeschwadern* – JG I (*Jastas* 4, 6, 10 and 11), JG II (*Jastas* 12, 13, 15 and 19), JG III (*Jastas* Boelcke, 26, 27 and 36), and JG IV (*Jastas* 23b, 32b, 34b and 35b). Volume Two will cover other D VII *Staffeln*.

Jasta 10 was apparently one of the first units to receive the new biplane at the beginning of May 1918. The *Jasta* was part of JG I, which was now commanded by Hptm Wilhelm Reinhard following the death of von Richthofen. JG I had first been formed on 24 June 1917, established as a permanent grouping of four *Jagdstaffeln* which would operate as a unit, and as such it was sent to various fronts to support a specific battle area. Due to the complexities of controlling large numbers of machines in the air in these days before aircraft radio, a *Jagdgeschwader* rarely operated in group strength – it would have been too unwieldy for one leader to command so large a force. It was more an administrative grouping, the *Geschwader* and its *staffeln* knowing that wherever it was posted, they all operated, even if only in *staffel* strength. During big battles at least two or three of the *staffeln* might operate together if possible.

The *Jagdgeschwader* should not be confused with the *Jagdgruppe*, which was a non-permanent formation of *Staffeln*. *Jagdgruppen* were generally created for a special purpose – to support a coming offensive or to operate with a specific army group, often for just short periods. They had a variety of numbers or names, the latter often relating to the name of the location or leader of such a formation – i.e. *Jagdgruppe* Lille or *Jagdgruppe* von Greim, which later became known as *Jagdgruppe* 10. Because the *Jagdgeschwadern* were moved about, and because of the German pilots' propensity to decorate their aircraft in bright colours, these units became known to the Allied airmen as 'Circuses', the most famous being JG I 'Richthofen Circus' – a name originally applied exclusively to *Jasta* 11.

JASTA 10

At the time of the Fokker D VII's arrival, *Jasta* 10 was the only unit of JG I still equipped with stationary-engined (and largely obsolete) Albatros D Va and Pfalz D IIIa fighters (as opposed to the rotary-engined Fokker Dr I). As such, it was the perfect candidate for early transition to the Mercedes-engined D VII. This famous unit was then commanded by Ltn Erich Löwenhardt, who – like the brothers Richthofen – came from Breslau. The son of a doctor, born on 7 April 1897, Löwenhardt was a former army cadet and infantry officer who had seen considerable action on the Eastern Front as a ski troop leader in the Carpathians.

Having earned the Iron Cross 1st Class for saving the lives of five wounded comrades, he then joined the air service, serving as an observer in 1916. Becoming a pilot, Löwenhardt had first flown in *Flieger Abteilung* (A) 265. He had joined *Jasta* 10 in March 1917, and was now its commander, his score of victories amounting to 18 by 2 May.

Jasta 10 apparently collected the Fokkers from the local air park as they became available, and for a short period the *Jasta* flew a mixture of its old yellow-nosed Albatros and Pfalz fighters along with the new D VIIs.

Löwenhardt had already proven himself as a talented *jagdflieger* with a thoughtful approach to aerial combat. Like other *Jasta* 10 pilots, he had given considerable thought to the dangerous task of balloon attacks, and counted eight such kills within his total. With the acquisition of the D VII, Löwenhardt's scoring rate would increase meteorically. He probably achieved his first kill in a D VII on 9 May. Richard Wenzl, who had joined *Jasta* 11 on 27 March, wrote in his book *Richthofen Flieger* (1930);

'In cheerful spirits, the *Geschwader* reassembled because a squadron had come into view near Albert. Now a second battle began (they had just had a scrap with some Camels – author). I headed high overhead and for the front in my splendid triplane. Already I was seeing the phosphorus play from the English observers' double-barreled machine guns and hearing their moaning. To my left, Löwenhardt in his new (D VII) biplane already had one in front of him. Rautter (of *Jasta* 4) and Kirschstein were working off to my right. My little fellow seemed to be a sure thing. Then suddenly my triplane started getting slower and slower and, to my surprise, the others pulled past me.'

Löwenhardt had downed an SE 5a near Hamel for his 19th victory, while the leader of JG I, Willi Reinhard (still flying a Dr I) destroyed a Camel for his 13th success. Löwenhardt claimed his 20th – a DH 4 – the next evening, and victory 21 fell on the 15th and victory 22 the following day. A Camel on the 18th followed by a balloon early on the 20th pushed his tally above the accepted number for the award of the *Pour le Mérite*, which he received on 31 May.

Gradually more D VIIs arrived at *Jasta* 10's airfield at Cappy, and on 20 May the unit moved to Etreux, near Guise, for a rest and to acquaint its pilots with the new aircraft. Karl Bodenschatz, JG I's adjutant, wrote in his book *Jagd in Flanderns Himmel* (1935);

'For five whole days there in Guise, the *Geschwader* can rest in peace. During this time, the new airfield at Puisieux Farm, five kilometres north-east of Laon, is being prepared. The machines are looked after. During these days off, some of the men familiarise themselves thoroughly with the new Fokker D VII, a biplane with a 160-hp Mercedes engine. Less manoeuvrable than the triplane, it is all the faster for it. If it climbs a little slow down below, it climbs surprisingly well higher up because its high-compression engine is designed for high altitudes.'

Löwenhardt continued to score at a rapid pace in his D VII with the bright yellow fuselage and tail, engaging in a friendly rivalry with Ernst Udet of *Jasta* 4 for the honour of top scorer of JG I. He frequently flew with *Jasta* 11 commander Lothar von Richthofen after the latter's return from convalescence on 19 July. As attrition decimated the experienced pilots of JG I, it fell to these veterans to shoulder most of the burden of the group's missions. Lothar wrote of these desperate days in his article 'My Last Time at the Front' (translated by Jan Hayzlett);

'I was flying with Löwenhardt and the best men from our two *Staffeln*. In my *Staffel*, things were looking very shaky. There was actually only one pilot who was any good. It was the same with Löwenhardt's *Staffel*. The best had fallen – the new pilots were good for very little. Flying with Löwenhardt was wonderful, almost like flying with Manfred. In just a short time we had become well-attuned to each other, and we could communicate splendidly with each other in the air. I was blessed, after Manfred, to have found again someone on whom I could depend. Löwenhardt expressed the same thing about me.'

Löwenhardt scored 16 victories in the intense battles of July to bring his score to 48, and a further five on 8 and 9 August raised this to 53. One of these on the 8th was JG I's 500th victory of the war. In addition, he was only the second German fighter pilot to reach 50 victories (Richthofen had been the first, and Udet would be the third) and at this time was the leading surviving *jagdflieger* in terms of victories.

Then came the fateful day of 10 August, just as the *Geschwader* had moved to Ennemain, west of St Quentin. Lothar wrote;

'Löwenhardt had sprained his ankle the day before. The next day, on the day of his death, the leg was all swollen. I told him that he should take his well-earned leave, that this was utter nonsense – he could barely stand. To no avail. We took off around 1100 hrs. That day we had also taken along all of the novice pilots. Löwenhardt was leading. There were about 12 aeroplanes, *Staffeln* 10 and 11 together (they sighted a British squadron coming directly toward them – author). Then a lone Englishman got through, a couple of hundred metres below us. Löwenhardt no doubt wanted to take him quick – the rest of the Englishmen could wait.

'He quickly put his machine on its nosé and attacked the lone single-seater. The whole horde of novice pilots went diving down after Löwenhardt, as if they all meant to shoot down that one Englishman. The scene was as follows – Löwenhardt in his bright yellow machine was right behind the Englishman. I saw right away that everyone else was superfluous. But four or five of them didn't realise this, and were flying right behind Löwenhardt. Then, all of a sudden, I see the Englishman dive straight down, a trail of smoke behind him . . . what's that? Löwenhardt is no longer flying behind the downed Englishman – just a chaotic mess of thousands of splinters.'

The *Jasta* 10 commander had collided with the D VII of Ltn Alfred Wentz of *Jasta* 11. According to Wentz's account, Löwenhardt's wheels had struck his upper right wing. A piece of fabric ripped from the wing, and Wentz lost control of his machine. Both pilots took to their parachutes. Wentz landed safely, but the great ace's chute failed to deploy and he fell to his death near Chaulnes at 1215 hrs. He was given credit for the SE 5a to bring his final score to 54.

Another successful *Jasta* 10 airman during the early Fokker D VII period was Ltn Friedrich 'Fritz' Friedrichs. Born on 21 February 1895 in Spark, Westphalia, he had hoped for a medical career but the war changed his plans. Friedrichs had been wounded in Serbia with the infantry, and upon being classified unfit he transferred into aviation. After a period on two-seaters, he arrived at *Jasta* 10 on 11 January 1918 but did not score until 21 March. By the end of May Friedrichs had six kills attained in Pfalz and Albatros fighters. In June, now flying the D VII, he downed eight balloons and five aircraft to bring his score to 19. Wenzl called him 'Löwenhardt's partner, the very capable Friedrichs, the tireless balloon killer'. In the first week of July he shot down two American-flown Nieuport 28 fighters to take his score to 21, which set the wheels in motion for the award of the *Pour le Mérite* – the yardstick at this time being 20 kills.

However, Friedrichs failed to return from a sortie on 15 July, and as the 'Blue Max' was not awarded posthumously, the award was never given. Flying D VII 309/18, Friedrichs was out on an evening sortie towards the Allied balloon lines. Suddenly, his Fokker burst into flames due to the unstable incendiary phosphorus ammunition used to ignite balloons.

On 10 August 1918 Oblt Erich Löwenhardt was killed when his bright yellow D VII collided with the Fokker flown by Alfred Wentz of *Jasta* 11. The *Jasta* 10 commander took to his parachute but the canopy failed to deploy. Here, his coffin lies in state at the *Staffel* airfield at Bernes, flanked by the lower wings of a D VII and an honour guard. The black velvet pillow (*Ordenkissen*) displays his 'Blue Max' above his other medals (*via VanWyngarden*)

Two formidable air fighters of *Jasta* 10. Ltn 'Fritz' Friedrichs (left) and his friend and CO, Ltn Erich Löwenhardt, pose with a captured SPAD XIII. Richard Wenzl called Friedrichs the 'tireless balloon killer', and the ace counted 16 balloons in his final tally of 21. Löwenhardt would achieve 54 confirmed claims before his accidental death on 10 August, placing him third on the list of all German World War 1 aces (*via VanWyngarden*)

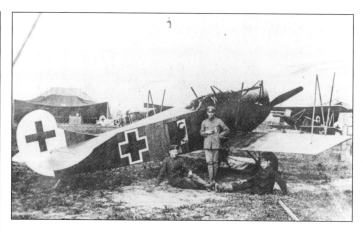

A *Jasta* 10 pilot thought to be Ltn Friedrichs poses with his groundcrew and his early production Fokker D VII with its 'streaky' camouflaged fuselage. This Fokker would have been marked with the yellow nose and wheel covers of *Jagdstaffel* 10, and was emblazoned with an unidentified crest marking on the fuselage. A band of unknown colour (blue?) also appears just ahead of the fuselage cross. Aloys Heldmann claimed that Friedrichs' aircraft were marked with the colours of Schleswig-Holstein, although the details and significance of this crest marking remain obscure. Friedrichs was a native Westphalian, but did serve for a time in a Schleswig-Holstein infantry regiment. Much about this aircraft remains unknown. On 15 July 1918 Friedrichs died when the volatile phosphorus ammunition in his D VII 309/18 ignited, setting the machine aflame. He took to his parachute, but the harness snagged on the aircraft's tail and the shroud lines broke *(via VanWyngarden)*

The ammunition was stored in a box close to the engine, and during the hot summer months it was prone to self-ignite, as it seems to have done so on this occasion – several other successful pilots would lose their lives due to this same problem. Friedrichs leapt from his burning machine but his parachute harness caught on the tailplane. The canopy deployed and the weight of both the aircraft and the pilot broke the shroud lines, and the ace was killed. As with his commander Löwenhardt, the balloon buster had fallen undefeated by the enemy.

As Friedrichs died, Ltn Justus Grassmann was just getting started. This 21-year-old had also been through the two-seater process, finally becoming a fighter pilot with *Jasta* 10 on 17 October 1917. He was even more of a slow starter than Friedrichs had been, only obtaining his first kill on 5 June 1918. Grassmann's first two claims were against balloons, but following his meagre scoring start, he went on to down ten aircraft and three balloons before the war ended. According to a letter he wrote in 1960, Grassmann's D VII bore the usual yellow nose of the *Staffel*, along with a brown and white striped tailplane and elevators as a personal marking.

Among Grassmann's claims were two Allied aces. On 28 July he had downed a Camel flown by Capt W S Stephenson DFC of No 73 Sqn, who became a prisoner – he had claimed his 12th victory earlier that day. Then on 11 August *Jasta* 10 became involved with Sopwith Dolphins of No 19 Sqn, two being shot down. Grassmann probably got the one flown by Capt G B Irving, a Canadian who was about to receive the DFC, and who had also achieved his 12th kill shortly before being downed himself.

The other Fokker pilot to destroy a Dolphin in this 11 August battle was Ltn Aloys Heldmann, another of *Jasta* 10's D VII aces. Heldmann was already an established ace, having achieved five victories before the D VIIs arrived. From Grevenbruch, near Cologne (born on 2 December 1895), he had been an engineering student pre-war. Heldmann transferred to the air service from the infantry following action on the Eastern Front, and on two-seaters he had seen operations on both the Eastern and Western Fronts, before becoming a fighter pilot.

Joining *Jasta* 10 in November 1916, Heldmann gradually learnt his trade, and due to his rank actually held temporary command of the *Jasta* twice in 1918. By the end of the war he had achieved 15 victories. After the war Heldmann returned to his engineering roots, but in 1933 he joined the Luftwaffe, and with the rank of colonel became an inspector of a flying school. Captured by the British at the end of the war, he later lived in Bad Aibling, Germany, and died in the 1980s.

Another Fokker ace with *Jasta* 10 was Arthur Laumann, who carried his initials 'AL' on his machine. Most of his victories came whilst serving with *Jasta* 66, having joined this unit in May 1918 after a period on two-seaters. Born in Essen on 4 July 1894, Laumann had been an artilleryman in the early part of the war. With *Jasta* 66 he had scored 23 victories by

11 August 1918, having become leader of the unit on 21 July. However, upon the death of Löwenhardt he was sent to JG I to command *Jasta* 10. His last five kills were all scored with this *Staffel*, bringing his score to 28.

Although his tally had reached 20 on 9 August, Laumann did not score again after 4 September (some records note 24 victories with *Jasta* 66, and only four with *Jasta* 10, the 28th being credited on 30 August), and it therefore took some time for his *Pour le Mérite* to be awarded. This came on 27 October 1918, and he was the last recipient of this prestigious award within the ranks of JG I. Laumann too joined the Luftwaffe, in 1935, and became CO of the new JG 2 '*Richthofen*' prior to World War 2. By the end of that war he was serving as air attaché to Yugoslavia and Greece. He died from a stroke in Münster on 18 November 1970.

Fellow ace Saxon-born Paul Aue had been with *Kampfstaffel* 30 of *Kampfgeschwader Nr.5* in 1916 after he had shown his talent for combat on 25 October of that year when he and his observer downed a British BE 2c near Bapaume. That same month he was assigned to *Jasta* 10.

His next two victories are obscure, but his fourth came on 25 March 1917. Aue was wounded on 19 September, at which time his score had

By September 1918 the Heinecke parachute harness had been widely issued, as this photo of *Jasta* 10 pilots ready for immediate take-off shows. These men are, from left to right, with known victories, Uffz Hennig, Ltns Schibilsky, Justus Grassmann (13) and Aloys Heldmann (15, and acting CO), Ofz Stv Paul Aue (10), Ltn Kohlbach (5), Uffz Klamt and Ltn Bähren. The D VII with its engine running in the background may be Heldmann's D VII (F) 4264/18 *(via VanWyngarden)*

This familiar Sanke postcard shows *Jasta* 10 leader Arthur Laumann's Fokker-built D VII emblazoned with his initials. The aircraft was covered in four-colour printed fabric, and would have displayed the *Staffel's* usual yellow décor. The colour of the background band of the 'AL' insignia is unknown, but just might have been light yellow as well. Note the tubular sight mounted between the guns *(via VanWyngarden)*

risen to five. By his own account, he refused to be taken away from the front despite his wound. By the time he returned to action in February 1918, Aue was flying the Albatros D V, and he gained his sixth victory on 3 May. Following the conversion to the D VII, he claimed four more kills to bring his tally to ten – a score he personally acknowledged after the war – plus three more unconfirmed. Aue was another to join the inter-war Luftwaffe in the 1930s and saw service during World War 2. He died in Russian captivity in 1945.

JAGDGESCHWADER I KOMMANDEURS

As mentioned already, Hptm Wilhelm Reinhard had been leader of JG I following von Richthofen's death. Born on 12 March 1891 in Dusseldorf, he had joined the military in 1909, serving in the artillery. Severely wounded in November 1914, Reinhard had just returned to the front when his transfer to aviation was confirmed. Flying two-seaters, he was wounded again in December 1915 but came back for more. Wanting to fly fighters, he reached *Jasta* 11 on 24 June 1917, just as JG I was formed. By the end of that year Reinhard had scored six kills.

Flying Dr Is in the first months of 1918, he brought his score to 12 as leader of *Jasta* 6. Once he became commander of JG I, he began to fly D VIIs, taking his tally to 20 on 12 June, and thus being eligible for the *Pour le Mérite*. However, Reinhard's death in a flying accident on 3 July precluded its actual award. This crash occurred during another evaluation by frontline pilots at Adlershof, Reinhard testing the Dornier-designed Zeppelin-Landau D I.

While there were undoubtedly a number of aces within JG I who seemed likely to take over command of the unit, only regular army career officers were judged to be fit to do so. As many pilots were only reserve officers, they were excluded from consideration. Therefore, eyes fell on Oblt Hermann Göring, *Staffelführer* of *Jasta* 27. To give him his due, Göring had been in action since the war began, both with the infantry and in the aviation service. He had flown as an observer, a two-seater pilot, in Eindeckers with two *Kampfeinsitzer Kommando* units (Keks), then served with *Jasta* 26. In May 1917 he had been given command of *Jasta* 27, which he had successfully led for over a year, and had 21 kills and the *Pour le Mérite*.

Today, it is difficult to be totally impartial about this man due to his subsequent history as one of Adolf Hitler's main henchmen, leader of the Luftwaffe and German Reichsmarschall. An examination of his combat claims reveals a number that appear suspect despite the rigorous confirmation routine that the German high command went through, and he is one of the very few to receive the *Pour le Mérite* in 1917 without the required 20 kills. There is no doubt he had a certain presence, and equally must have had friends in the right quarters, even in these early days.

Göring was given command of the prestigious JG I Richthofen on 8 July 1918, a fact that Richard Wenzl mentions in his book;

'Our new commander had arrived during our last days in Beugneux, Oblt Göring, the former leader of *Jasta* 27. If there had been some friction now and then during Reinhard's time, Göring understood how to make himself at home in the *Geschwader* in short order. He was a good comrade to us to the last and a good commander, who upheld the traditions of the *Geschwader*.'

As leader of *Jasta* 27 Göring had already flown two D VIIs, noted as 278/18 and 324/18. He gained his 19th, 20th and 21st victories in these machines. With JG I, it is well recorded that Göring achieved his 22nd and final victory on 18 July, flying D VII (F) 294/18 – this machine bore *Jasta* 11's red colour on its forward fuselage and a yellow tail as a personal marking. His most famous Fokker was the all-white D VII (F) 5125/18. What is also well documented is that as leader of perhaps the most famous unit in the German Air Service, he only gained one victory in this period – the French SPAD downed on 18 July.

Göring was on leave between 26 July and 22 August – an odd time to go just as he had been given command – and his last leave began on 22 October. While one must assume he did some flying in September and October, he gained no further kills. It could be argued, of course, that in four years he had done more than his share already, and he felt his primary duty as *Geschwader* commander was administrative leadership from the ground.

Oblt Hermann Göring, the final *Kommandeur* of JG I, strikes a typical pose with his red and white D VII (F), thought to be 4253/18 (previously flown by Udet). When Göring took over this BMW-engined machine, he had the rear fuselage painted in his personal white colour, while the forward fuselage was *Jasta* 11 red. This aircraft was equipped with sheet metal baffles on the coaming in front of the cockpit to deflect spent cartridges away from the pilot's immediate field of vision. Note also the tubular sight and the cut-down cockpit rim. The latter was probably effected to facilitate ease of entry, as Göring suffered from arthritis, aggravated by an old hip wound *(HAC/UTD via GVW)*

JASTA 11

Jagdstaffel 11 is the most famous German fighter unit of the Great War, due in no small part to Manfred von Richthofen. While the Rittmeister was dead by the time

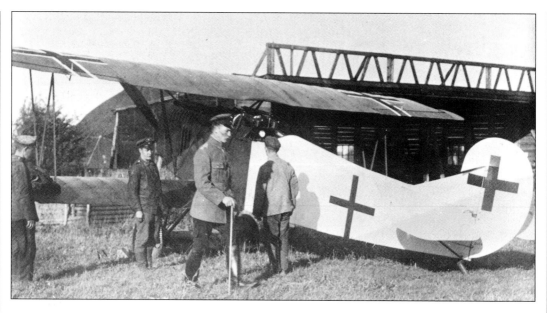

this illustrious *Staffel* was equipped with Fokker biplanes, it is perhaps fitting that the unit would be commanded for most of its D VII period by his younger – but no less formidable – brother, Lothar.

Lothar von Richthofen, from Breslau, was born on 27 September 1894. Like Manfred, he had started out in the cavalry, but transferred to aviation in the summer of 1915. Lothar joined his brother in *Jasta* 11 on 10 March 1917 and soon became just as deadly as Manfred, although he fought with a little more exuberance and recklessness than his more methodical brother. When he was wounded in the crash of his Dr I on 13 March 1918, he had 29 victories and the *Pour le Mérite.* Returning to the *Geschwader* in July, he downed his 30th victory – and the 500th kill for JG I – on the 25th of that month, in an unfamiliar D VII which he had borrowed from another pilot. In recalling this day, he later wrote;

'Arriving at the front at an altitude of 3000 to 4000 metres, I see roughly 100 enemy aircraft approaching, flying together with the utmost skill. Misty weather – thick fog hung in the air, making it very difficult to see. I now tried attacking the last of the enemy aeroplanes so as to not have

A fine view of Oblt Göring and his BMW-engined D VII (F) (probably 4253/18), which he flew as CO of the Richthofen *Geschwader*. The nose, struts and wheel covers were painted in the red colour of *Jagdstaffel* 11, while the remainder of the fuselage was white. The wings retained their printed camouflage fabric finish *(HAC/UTD via GVW)*

Göring's final D VII took his personal identification pattern to the extreme. D VII (F) 5125/18 was entirely white, except for the typical factory stencilling and national insignia. Its immaculate finish and precisely applied markings indicate that this aircraft was painted at the Fokker factory especially for Göring – Anthony Fokker and the JG I commander were good friends. This D VII was tested and accepted on 11 September 1918, and probably reached the *Geschwader* a week or two later. Again, the cockpit rim was cut down and a handle attached just forward of it *(via VanWyngarden)*

The so-called *Geschwader-Stock* was a traditional symbol of authority passed down from Richthofen, and Göring poses proudly with it. Behind him, a flare pistol tube protrudes from the fuselage, along with a rack for cartridges. The JG I leader wears the strengthened version of the Heinecke parachute harness *(via VanWyngarden)*

anyone behind me. Having reached the enemy, I look around and what is *not* behind me is my *Staffel*. The *Staffel* was no doubt coming up behind me but it was too far away to be able to take part in the coming fight. So I'll just show them how it's done.

'Three separate English single-seaters are flying in front and above me. In front and beneath me, a big squadron of French two-seaters flying close together – about 20 machines. I couldn't dive into that by myself, so I took aim at the middlemost machine of those overhead. I must have hit it with my very first rounds. The machine plunged and then caught itself again after 50 metres, but was out of control. I used up my remaining cartridges on the fellow, just in case. He should have burned but he didn't because I didn't even have any incendiary ammunition with me, which I didn't know. Still, I saw the impact.

'But stop! Where am I? I've lost my bearings! I want to fly back towards the sun as I'm just about to be attacked from above by an English single-seater. From overhead, he already has the advantage – I don't have any more ammunition anyway. There is nothing to be seen of my *Staffel*, so I'll have to let him shoot at me, try not to offer him an easy target, and

This classic study of Lothar von Richthofen and his father, Maj Albrecht von Richthofen, provides a fine view of Ltn Aloys Heldmann's D VII 244/18 of *Jasta* 10. This machine bore Heldmann's markings, but *Jasta* 11 commander von Richthofen was using it here. There is a suggestion that this photograph was taken on 25 July 1918 when Lothar recorded his 30th victory, as he is known to have been flying an unfamiliar, borrowed, D VII on this occasion. However, he claimed in his post-war writing that his father was unaware he was at the front that day! D VII 244/18 had the *Jasta* 10 yellow nose, and a personal black/white chequerboard tailplane and elevators. What was previously thought to be an 'AH' monogram painted on the top wing is now thought to be merely fabric repair. Note the streaked camouflage on the fuselage, rudder and fin, and the early 'thick' *Jasta* 10 style *Balkenkreuze* on those same components *(via VanWyngarden)*

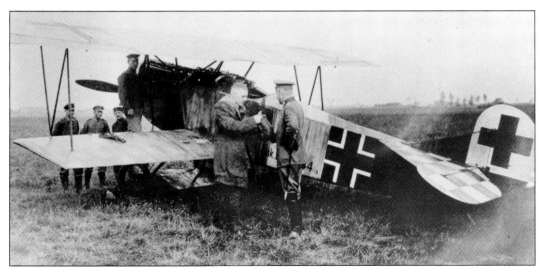

work my way back towards the front during the fight, so I'll be able to land behind our lines in case of a shot to the engine. After the Englishman has fired roughly 100 rounds at me, for some inexplicable reason he suddenly lets me go.'

Moments later von Richthofen was attacked again, and once more his enemy let him escape. He had probably downed a No 73 Sqn Camel.

Between 1 and 13 August Lothar von Richthofen went on to down another ten aircraft. For a time he flew a D VII he called 'my lovely red bird' – he downed two British aircraft with it on 8 August, then unfortunately broke its wing by taxiing into a tent in a careless landing. Nonetheless, he then borrowed Erich Just's machine and brought down his third British fighter of the day. On the 12th he downed two Camels from No 209 Sqn – the unit involved in the controversial demise of his brother. The two pilots shot down were Capt John K Summers MC, victor in eight combats, and Lt Kenneth Mac K Walker, who often flew with Summers, and with whom he had shared three of his five victories. Walker was killed, Summers made a prisoner of war. Lothar recorded;

'I went flying with (Erich) Just, (Eberhardt) Mohnicke and my cousin Ulf (Wolfram von Richthofen). Arriving at the front at an altitude of 4000 to 5000 metres, we see that it's swarming with Englishmen in every direction – only they were a good deal higher. Suddenly, we were attacked by seven or eight Camels. I got my hands on one which was attacking one of my companions with particular impudence. After scarcely 20 rounds, it started to burn and disappeared into the depths, burning till it reached the ground. Just and my cousin each bagged one as well.

'I then spotted another Camel just as its pilot commenced his attack from behind. A quick turn and a somewhat longer fight ensued. I noticed right away that I was dealing with no novice. What's more, he was the so-called "pennant man", meaning that on each wing, right and left, he carried a long pennant, usually in national colours. The aircraft in question was always the lead aeroplane. The fellow flew with exceptional skill, with the result that I hardly had a decent chance to fire. As soon as I got behind him and wanted to start firing, he made a tight turn and fired on me.

'Throughout this dogfight, we were going lower and lower. This gave me the advantage because we were quite a way this side of the lines. Just 500 metres above the ground, he tried his last trick to escape me. In such a case, which is considered equal to surrendering, you usually let your opponent be. I knew that old trick only too well though, because someone had already given me the slip once, in the same way. So I stayed close behind him and, sure enough, at an altitude of 10 metres, he once again tried to escape. So the chase continues. I don't have too many more cartridges, so I conserve them. I only fire single rounds from the one machine gun that still fired. In the process, as he later told me,

Jasta 11 *Staffelführer* Lothar von Richthofen (left) and Ltn Otto Förster (*Jasta* 11 adjutant) informally pose with a D VII. The aircraft appears to have borne a dark finish – it is tempting to suggest that this was Lothar's 'lovely red bird' which he was flying on 8 August, only to taxi it into a tent and break the wing *(via VanWyngarden)*

I shot right past his ear and shot his right machine gun sight to bits. Because of that, he then landed.

'I flew home. There I climbed into the car to drive over to where I'd brought him down. After some searching I find him and brought him back to our airfield where, three hours later, after parting from his comrades he sat down to a pleasant cup of tea. He stayed with us till the next morning – Capt Summers, 23 years old. Over the other side, he'd been a flight commander, and had already shot down a good many aeroplanes – how many he wouldn't say.'

Next day, the 13th, Lothar took to the air again. He had already been twice wounded on the foreboding 13th of the month, and would not have had to fly this day as he had some administrative affairs to deal with. 'But no – today the spell of the 13th had to be broken'.

He was chasing a two-seater and saw the observer go down under his fire. Looking over his shoulder to ensure that he was being covered by his pilots, he was surprised to find several Camels coming down on him. He broke away and half rolled, but a bullet hit his leg. Losing height, he managed to force-land in the Somme battleground. Von Richthofen had been attacked by American pilots of the 148th Aero Squadron, and may have been the victim of Lt Field Kindley, who claimed a D VII 'out of control' north of Roye, or by Lt George V Siebold who made a similar claim. Lothar spent the rest of the war recuperating from his wound.

After the war Lothar tried to go into farming and then went into industry. In June 1919 he married Doris, Countess von Keyserlingk, and they had two children before the marriage was dissolved. Finally he returned to flying, taking mail and passengers between Berlin and Hamburg. On 4 July 1922, while approaching Hamburg, the engine of his LVG C VI aircraft failed. In the crash which followed, two passengers were injured and Lothar died on the way to hospital.

Mention of the third von Richthofen in one of Lothar's accounts brings us to the brothers' distant cousin, Wolfram Ulf von Richthofen. Born at Barzdorf, Silesia, on 11 October 1895, he was a year younger than Lothar, but like his famous relatives he too served at first in the cavalry from 1913, and at the start of the war saw action in Russia and France. He transferred to aviation in early 1917, and it is hardly surprising that Manfred had him posted to his *Jasta* 11 at the beginning of April 1918. His first actions were in a Fokker Dr I, famously in the fight which ended in Manfred's death on 21 April. In that skirmish he was attacked by another tyro fighter pilot, Wilfred May of No 209 Sqn. Manfred, seeing Wolfram under attack, dived on May and began the chase which ended in his fall on the Morlancourt Ridge.

Wolfram gained his first victory on 4 June and his second five days later. By the end of the war he had eight kills, most if not all on the D VII. After the war he went into engineering, but like so many other wartime airmen, signed up with the pre-World War 2 Luftwaffe, and was Chief of Staff to the *Kondor Legion* in Spain. Von Richthofen attained the rank of Generalfeldmarschall in World War 2, having led a Stuka dive-bomber *gruppe* in Poland, France and on the Russian Front, and commanded *Luftflotte* 2 in Italy in 1943-44. A brain tumor curtailed his war, and shortly after being taken prisoner by the Americans after VE-Day, he died of a brain haemorrhage on 12 June 1945.

Ltn d R Erich Just affects an informal attitude for this photograph with his *Jasta* 11 D VII. This machine seems to have been finished in four-colour printed fabric, and displayed the unit's red nose, wheels and struts. Just's personal emblem was the black(?) and white sash on the fuselage, in the proportions of the iron cross ribbon. He probably attained his final three victories in a D VII, and was one of those competent and reliable pilots who formed the backbone of the *Jasta*. After wrecking his own D VII on 8 August, Lothar von Richthofen borrowed Just's Fokker (perhaps this very one?) to obtain his third victory of the day
(A Imrie via HAC/UTD)

Vzfw Willi Gabriel adopts an intimidating pose alongside his *Jasta* 11 Fokker D VII 286/18. He described the finish of this machine to historian Alex Imrie many years ago, and it remains the classic example of a *Jasta* 11 D VII. When this photograph was taken, the fighter bore the unit's red colour on the engine cowling and cabane struts only. The rest of the fuselage was in the usual streaked olive-brown finish seen on early Fokker-built machines. Gabriel followed standard *Jasta* 11 practice in applying his individual colours to the tail section – orange and sky blue stripes. In time the aircraft would bear additional lengthwise orange stripes on the fuselage sides and top decking *(A Imrie via GVW)*

Ltn Erich Just scored his first victories with *Jasta* 11 in a Dr I, but his third through to his sixth were attained with the D VII. Born in 1898, he was assigned to *Jasta* 11 on 20 September 1917. Wounded twice in combat before going onto the D VII, Just survived the war.

One of the more interesting and colourful aces in *Jasta* 11 was Willi Gabriel, whose twin brother Walter was also a pilot. Both boys had been interested in aviation as youngsters, so it was natural for them to join the air service once war came.

Born in Bromberg on the last day of 1893, the twins were sons of a furniture manufacturer. As teenagers, they built their own aeroplane in 1912 and managed to fly it. Both flew two-seaters in the early days, and although Walter managed a brief stint as a fighter pilot, he was soon back on two-seaters and was then taken prisoner on 19 August 1917, flying a Rumpler.

Willi, meanwhile, enjoyed a more adventurous war by flying with *Schlachtstaffel* 15, whose job it was to attack enemy infantry on the ground. On 22 March he and his observer shot down a SPAD two-seater, which only whetted his appetite for combat, and he actually asked Manfred von Richthofen (whose JG I shared the airfield with his unit) if he could transfer. Gabriel's CO managed to block the transfer, but after von Richthofen's death Gabriel tried again, and this time Reinhard swung it. Willi became a fighter pilot with *Jasta* 11 on 19 May 1918.

Upon his arrival, Reinhard told Vzfw Gabriel that despite his experience, if he failed to shoot down any hostile aircraft within four weeks he was being returned to his previous unit. Reinhard need not have worried. Gabriel talked himself onto the evening patrol of his first day and shot down a DH 9 of No 49 Sqn. He could stay!

In June, flying a D VII, Gabriel shot down two balloons and two Allied fighters, but upon the arrival of Hermann Göring as *Geschwader Kommandeur*, he quickly ran into trouble. Göring had his own ideas on how things should be done, which differed from those of the previous

This perspective of Gabriel's 286/18 provides a fine look at its orange and sky blue tail chevrons. Also evident is the streaked camouflage on the fuselage and the style of exhaust exit. The wings were covered in five-colour printed fabric. Gabriel had a spectacular, but brief, career with *Jasta* 11, achieving a quadruple victory on 18 July to bring his score to 11. By that time he was no longer flying the machine seen here, but a BMW-engined D VII. His 'lone hunter' tactics that day, and his disregard for Göring's orders, earned him a posting to an air park for the rest of the war (*A Imrie via GVW*)

leaders of JG I. Reinhard in particular had not frowned on experienced pilots flying lone patrols, but Göring was against this. In truth he was probably right. Gone were the days of the loners, and even if they had some successes, it was often just a matter of time before they ran into something they could not handle and were shot down.

Not that Gabriel had any great love for Reinhard. The *Geschwader* leader was nearing his 20th victory, and the 'Blue Max', on 12 June when both he and Gabriel attacked a SPAD two-seater, which was downed. Karl Bodenschatz, the adjutant, asked Gabriel not to pursue his claim and let Reinhard have the credit. German pilots did not share victories as in other air forces, and if a kill was disputed, it went to arbitration for a final decision on who should get the credit, unless one pilot withdrew.

Gabriel refused, having lost a similar claim a few weeks previously, and had been told the next joint claim would go in his favour. Medals, fame and promotion followed victories for successful fighter pilots, and every pilot capable of downing enemy machines was keen to share in this success. With Reinhard about to leave for the fighter trials in Berlin, Bodenschatz pleaded once more to the NCO pilot, promising that if he withdrew the claim, the next two disputes would go in his favour. Reluctantly Gabriel did as he was asked, and then, of course, Reinhard was killed at the fighter trials, so it would not have mattered in any event.

Now with Göring's new directive, Gabriel was again aggrieved. His peace of mind was not improved on 26 June when he saw friend, and ten-victory ace, Werner Steinhäuser shot down as he flew alongside Gabriel's machine. Steinhäuser, who would have celebrated his 25th birthday in three days time, had been hit in the head and killed instantly. Gabriel had to watch the yellow and red-tailed Fokker go into a succession of dives and zooms as it slowly lost height before finally crashing into a wood.

On 18 July Gabriel flew on a patrol led by Göring, and although there had been a brief fight with some SPADs, nothing was claimed. As the patrol returned to base, Gabriel decided to turn and take another look over the trenches. Spotting another formation of SPADs, he climbed up

21

behind them, and taking careful aim on the rearmost, shot it down. The other SPAD pilots went for him, and in the fight which followed Gabriel shot down another, this one in flames, and as he headed into German territory the rest broke off – much to his relief.

Heading back to base, he knew Göring would be far from happy, but hoped his two kills might placate the *Kommandeur*. Then he saw three Bréguet XIV two-seaters. As he began to head for them, he noticed another Fokker D VII also about to attack. Gabriel was flying one of the new BMW-engined Fokkers, and being light on fuel at this stage of the sortie, his machine was not only lighter but faster than the other D VII.

The other German pilot, it transpired, was Richard Wenzl, now flying with *Jasta* 6, and in his Mercedes-engined Fokker he watched as Gabriel roared past him to make his first attack. In his memoirs, Wenzl claimed that he had already attacked the Bréguet and silenced its rear gunner, and that Gabriel robbed him of his rightful victory. At any rate, Gabriel's attack was made almost over the *Geschwader* airfield, and he knew that everyone would be watching as the three Bréguets had closed up in anticipation of an attack. Gabriel closed in and fired at one of the two-seaters, then attacked again. This time the pilot too seemed to have been hit. The machine began a spin earthwards, Gabriel watching until it ploughed into the ground just one kilometre from the field.

Putting down at base, he was congratulated by all on this victory, but then he told them he had already downed two SPADs beforehand. Göring, however, was far from pleased with the brash NCO who dared to disobey his instructions and go off on his own. Apparently Göring then told Gabriel to confirm his own SPAD kill in the earlier fight, but Gabriel, having not seen any such thing, refused.

In an afternoon patrol Gabriel, still feeling somewhat rebellious, again broke formation and went hunting alone, hoping to prove Göring wrong. In fact he sped low across the lines as he had done when a *Schlasta* pilot. Then, in the haze, he spotted a SPAD two-seater and two single-seater escorts. He attacked the two-seater and watched it crash into the battle area, the two SPAD fighters heading up and away, apparently fleeing.

Back at base Göring was furious. This flagrant breach of discipline was not something he would tolerate, and despite four victories in one day, Gabriel was grounded and given four weeks leave. He was told to fly an aircraft to the local aircraft park for overhaul, but instead he carried on and flew the Albatros D Va all the way back to Germany. With no flight authorisation, Göring was in trouble too, and when finally Gabriel returned to the *Geschwader* on 20 August, he was given a severe reprimand and then posted as a test pilot to an aircraft park. His war was over.

After the war both Gabriel brothers still worked with their home-built aeroplanes, flying joy-ride and charter flights. Called up for reserve training in 1935, Willi flew Heinkel He 51s. In 1938 he flew a Fokker Dr I and a D VII in two films. In World War 2 Gabriel rose to the rank of hauptmann, flying Ju 88s and Me 210s.

Oblt Erich Rudiger von Wedel joined *Jasta* 11 on 23 April 1918, only two days after Richthofen's death. His transfer to the unit had been arranged by the Rittmeister himself, as the two were old comrades who had served in the same Uhlan regiment at the war's start. Von Wedel would never have the opportunity to fly with his old friend, but he was obviously imbued with leadership qualities, for even before claiming his first victory on 10 May he was acting commander of the *Jasta.* This was followed by another stint in July and August. Finally, on 31 August, by which time von Wedel's score had risen to ten, he was given full command. On 5 November 1918 he downed his 13th and last kill. He died in 1954.

Another experienced fighter ace to join *Jasta* 11 late in the war was Friedrich Noltenius, who had achieved 15 victories with *Jasta* 27 and *Jasta* 6. However, after a clash with *Jasta* 6 commander Ulrich Neckel, he moved across to *Jasta* 11. His exploits in *Jasta* 27 will be detailed later. With *Jasta* 11 he brought his score to 21 on 4 November 1918, a total which included eight balloons. Noltenius' first three claims with *Jasta* 11 were all made on 23 October – two balloons and a SPAD. His last combat, on 4 November, was against DH 4s of the US 11th Aero Squadron, and he downed one and possibly another which was not credited nor confirmed. In his diary Noltenius noted;

'I saw flak bursts at the Maas – a bomber formation! I hurried in its direction, saw a two-seater returning and cut off its retreat by diving in front of it. He shot desperately with the gun protruding through the bottom of the fuselage, but without taking aim of course. I scored a hit in his fuel tank. Meanwhile, Schulte (Ltn Julius Schulte-Frohlinde, four kills – author) had approached from the other side and now was closer than I as he did not have to evade the enemy's fire. The DH went up in flames.

'As soon as I saw it burning, I turned off in the direction of the main formation, where we met head-on over Carignan. Weaving heavily, I passed by the ten DHs with a smart turn, and positioned myself behind the rearmost one. In a longer battle I first shot him smoking, and then shot his engine to pieces. This slowed him down. Then I got nearer and shot him down in flames. Thereupon I immediately attacked the next one. Under my fire he developed a petrol vapour trail, but then I caught a bullet in the radiator and had to break off because I could not see a thing in the steam cloud. I landed at the field of JG II.

'Later I learned from an officer who had observed the battle from the ground that the last one I had attacked had crashed also. But this information came much later as reports from the ground came only rarely in those days of the retreat.'

Oblt Erich Rüdiger von Wedel had been a comrade of Manfred von Richthofen's in his old Uhlan regiment. Though his transfer to *Jasta* 11 was arranged by the Baron, he ironically arrived at the *Staffel* two days after his friend's death. Von Wedel went on to down 13 aircraft and became the last commander of *Jagdstaffel* 11 (HAC/UTD via GVW)

THE BMW ENGINE

The BMW IIIa engine of 185-hp made a marked improvement in the performance of the already superior Fokker D VII. This could often give the edge to the German fighter pilots, especially if engaged by Allied pilots used to fighting the Mercedes-engined D VIIs who suddenly found themselves at a distinct disadvantage. As Gabriel had found on the occasion in which he attacked the three Bréguets, he left Wenzl, in a 160-hp Mercedes machine, standing. In actual fact, he and Gabriel had to roll the dice for this victory, and Wenzl lost.

Such was the increase in performance of the BMW Fokkers that everyone was keen to get them as quickly as possible. Hermann Göring wrote to *Kofl.* 7 (*Kommandeur der Flieger* of the 7. *Armee*) on 20 July 1918;

'Now that two *Staffeln* of the *Geschwader* are equipped with the newly released BMW IIIa engines, it is obviously apparent that it is an urgent necessity to get the entire *Geschwader* equipped with these engines as soon as possible. The BMW engine is better than the Mercedes (particularly at greater altitude). It is this fact that does not allow the cooperation of all four *Staffeln*, or permit them to fly as one unit. If we are to continue without the great advantages of the BMW engines, this cannot be done. Both in speed and in climb rate, the Mercedes and BMW do not compare.

'The first two *Staffeln* usually succeed in climbing and engaging the enemy squadrons but the other two remain behind, and thus only half of the combat capability of the *Geschwader* is utilised. A uniform attack is not possible. Being aware of this fact arouses great discontent with the pilots who do not have the BMW engine, especially if they see their comrades, with their superior performance, able to engage and score without themselves being able to attack. Such a close unit as the Richthofen *Geschwader*, which is always assigned to the main fighting fronts, must be uniformly equipped with the best and most modern material available. I therefore, please, again ask for accelerated delivery of BMW engines.'

On 2 August, Göring wrote again;

'The BMW IIIa engine continues to perform splendidly. Apart from some small deficiencies which are already remedied, nothing has turned out to be unfavourable. Its superiority as compared to the other engines (also the enemy's) is proven daily. Generally the "over gas" throttle position is not used under 3000 metres. Not only have we been operating in the "over gas" throttle position almost constantly throughout aerial engagements, but also at low altitude, and without any damage to the engine (only stronger vibration becomes apparent).

'Recently, a pilot, after being pressed down near a captive balloon, was attacked by some SPADs. He flew for over half an hour with the throttle in the "over gas" position and the motor at full revs (1500-1600 rpm) at a height of 100 metres, pursued by the SPADs. It was superior in rate to the SPADs. The engine operated smoothly and had not suffered in the slightest. Again the *Geschwader* requests it for immediate delivery and recommends (since an immediate and extensive supply of this engine is needed as soon as possible), that factories under licence do not ignore the demand.'

Four days later, Lothar von Richthofen, in temporary command of the *Geschwader*, wrote;

'I. *Performance*. The BMW engine is a great advancement in the design of aircraft motors. Through increased over-compression, larger bore of the cylinders, and a first-class carburettor (which was designed particularly for higher altitudes), the Bavarian Motor Works has succeeded in manufacturing a motor which makes our D-aeroplanes superior to all types of enemy aircraft at higher altitudes.

'Up to 2000 metres, the BMW motor operates insignificantly better than the over-compressed 160-hp Mercedes motor. However, as soon as the "over gas" throttle position is engaged, the performance of the BMW motor is greatly superior to the over-compressed 160-hp Mercedes. On average, 5000 metres in 17-20 minutes, and 6000 metres in 23-36 minutes, were achieved.

'II. *Mode of operation of the BMW motor*. The vibration from the over compression is no more violent than the Albatros D V aeroplane with a 160-hp Mercedes. The vibration could be dampened by using a somewhat stronger motor mount in the Fokker D VII.

'In order to not unnecessarily stress the motor, and maintain the advantage, the "over gas" throttle position should be used only above 2000 metres with direct climbing or in aerial combat. It is absolutely necessary that each pilot is instructed in the mode of operation of the BMW motor (in order to avoid unnecessary motor failure).

'As soon as all *Staffeln* are equipped with BMW aircraft, I suggest sending additional reserve motors in the ratio of two for every 20 D VIIs.'

On the day before Göring again left on leave (2 September), he wrote the following technical report;

'Lately, the *Geschwader* has succeeded in regaining complete domination of the sky. The enemy is much more on the defensive and is usually out of reach and at a great altitude. The superiority of the Fokker D VII with the BMW IIIa motor has increased quickly. We have succeeded several times in surprising the enemy by staying low, and as we approach, fly closely to him, then suddenly apply "over gas" throttle, quickly climb over and thus gain the better tactical position. Likewise, since the *Geschwader* has been equipped with the BMW engines, it has been easier to climb and catch the enemy squadrons. The Fokker D VII with the BMW is equal to all other aircraft types at diving ability, and superior to the 300-hp SPADs. It must be reiterated, the fastest introduction and supply of the BMW engine is desired, therefore enabling other *Staffeln* to continue to be important tools in shooting down enemy aircraft.'

Despite Göring's – and others' – urgent request for BMW engines, German factories were obviously not able, at this stage of the war, to produce them in numbers that would satisfy demand. Even as late as 1 November 1918, Göring was pursuing production of the 185-hp motors;

'By production and introduction of the BMW IIIa motor, the German fighter has become equal, or frequently superior, to the best enemy single-seaters. This high altitude motor is a great advancement over all past motors. Each fighter pilot urgently requires a BMW motor.'

JASTA 4

After his brief stint with *Jasta* 11 in the spring of 1918, in which he brought his score to 23, Ernst Udet became CO of *Jasta* 4 on 20 May. He had just recently been awarded the *Pour le Mérite* and had become engaged to Eleonore 'Lo' Zink, whose nickname adorned his aircraft.

Jasta 4 was the last of the *Geschwader* units to be equipped with the D VII, in mid-June, by which time Udet had raised his score to 28. Born on 26 April 1896 in Frankfurt-am-Main, he was still only 21 when he received the 'Blue Max' on 9 April 1918. Udet had begun his war as a motorcyclist with the 26th Württemburg Reserve Division in 1914. However, an accident ended his cycling career and he applied for a transfer to the air service, which he finally achieved in December 1915. As a lowly gefreiter pilot, he flew two-seaters, earning the Iron Cross 2nd class, and then began flying Eindeckers with a Kek unit.

Udet gained his first combat victory on 18 March 1916 when he downed a French bomber raiding Mülhausen – a feat which brought him the Iron Cross 1st class. He was then assigned to *Jasta* 15, gained two more kills and received a commission. With his score at six, Udet moved to *Jasta* 37, which he later commanded. By June 1918, flying D VIIs in *Jasta* 4, his score began to increase even more rapidly as he started his competition with his friend Löwen-hardt. By the end of that month he had a total of 36 victories, and on 3 July it reached 40.

After the war Udet recorded how the 160 hp-engined D VII was losing its advantage over Allied fighters as 1918 progressed, especially above 13,000 ft. When finally 22 D VIIs with the BMW engines arrived at *Jasta* 11, during the French advance between Reims and Soissons, Udet was able to persuade Göring to let

him have two of these machines for his *Staffel*. During his first flight in one Udet was amazed at the remarkable increase in power over the Mercedes-engined D VIIs, the engine being smooth and easily throttled down. He remembered the day – 29 June – for he was later shot down that same day in his famous Mercedes D VII marked with the striped upper wing and the impudent legend *Du doch nicht!!* on the elevators.

Udet had attacked a Bréguet, keeping just below its tail so the observer could not target him. He fired and saw the observer crumple into the cockpit. Thinking he had taken care of the rear gunner, he then came at the Bréguet from the side to complete the job. However, as he wrote in his book *Mein Fliegerleben*;

'I have closed in to about 20 metres when the observer appears behind his machine gun, ready to fire. In a moment it rattles about my head as though pebbles were falling onto a metal tabletop. My Fokker rears like a shying horse and turns into a sitting duck. The elevator is shot up, its attachment to the stick is severed and the cable flaps in the propwash.

'My machine is shot lame, drooping to the left and circling – I can't steer it. Below me is the torn landscape, being turned over anew by the impact of new shells. There is only one possibility of getting back. Every time the Fokker heads east, I carefully open the throttle. In this way the circles are elongated, and I can hope to work my way back to our lines.

Udet appears third from the right (face just turned to the camera) in this candid shot of a *Jasta* 4 group at Bernes airfield in August 1918. Most intriguing, however, is Udet's rarely seen D VII (OAW) on the far right. It bore only a factory finish of four-colour printed fabric, plus Udet's usual white chevron emblem on the tail and, of course, his 'LO!' talisman on the fuselage. The black/white borders on the fuselage longerons and the black nose, wheels and struts were typical *Jasta* 4 markings, and this machine also had black/white streamers on the tail. This D VII line-up also includes von Gluszewski's machine fifth from right, and sixth is Richard Kraut's (HAC/UTD)

Friendly rivals in *Jagdgeschwader* I, Erich Löwenhardt (left) of *Jasta* 10 and Ernst Udet of *Jasta* 4 engaged in an amicable scoring competition in the summer of 1918, much to the detriment of their opponents. Udet is also engaging in a bit of a masquerade here – he is wearing a captured British observer's uniform, complete with fleece-lined thigh boots (not visible) and winged 'O' insignia! The good-natured horseplay evident here belies the fact that these were two of the deadliest of all World War 1 pilots, credited with a combined 116 confirmed Allied aircraft shot down. In the background is a *Jasta* 6 D VII, possibly Richard Wenzl's machine (HAC/UTD via GVW)

'It is a slow, tortuous process, but suddenly the machine stands on end and dives straight down like a rock. Parachute – pull up the legs – stand on the seat! In a moment the air pressure throws me to the rear. A blow in my back - I am stuck to the rudder. The straps of the parachute harness, secured too loosely, have become fouled with the elevator, and the falling machine is dragging me along with irresistible force. "Lo will cry", I think. "My mother". I will be unrecognisable – I have no papers on me.

'I attempt, with all my strength, to bend back the elevator. It is hard, terribly hard. Then, a jerk, I am free! I float down on the straps like a swimmer. Immediately afterwards, a jolt, I have landed. The parachute opened at the last moment.'

Udet's landing was a violent one, and he sprained his left ankle, but his ordeal was not over. He freed himself from the parachute and began a long run through the midst of an artillery bombardment, some of it in poison gas shells. After having been thrown to the ground by the blast of a shell, he finally found safety with an infantry regiment, though he 'suffered violent coughing and retching as I had covered some three kilometres without a gas mask'. He was eventually picked up by a *Geschwader* car and – nerves intact – flew another sortie that same afternoon.

The next day Udet flew his red BMW Fokker for the first time in combat and found he had to constantly throttle back so that his *Staffel* pilots could keep up with him. Nevertheless, he shot down a SPAD that same evening with apparent ease – in fact, he shot down four more aircraft in the next three days. The other BMW D VII he gave to Heinrich Drekmann. Both men often flew over the Allied lines above 19,000 ft without being seen, and from here they were able to surprise many French aircraft by diving on them from the west. A letter taken from a French PoW even described a red Fokker which had attacked several of his comrades' aircraft within their own lines;

'Furthermore, this red-painted machine has been talked about several times recently. In any event, in it sits a pilot equal to our Fonck.'

In the first half of August Udet was even more prolific. During the great battles over the British offensive, which began on 8 August (the Battle of Amiens), he added 20 more victories to his tally by the 22nd – part of this time he was acting commander of the *Geschwader*, following Lothar von Richthofen's wounding and with Göring still on leave.

One of these victories, on the evening of 8 August, was not so much from his fire as from his closeness of attack, as he later wrote;

'South of Foucaucourt I meet two. One immediately takes off westward – the other remains. He rains propaganda leaflets on me from above. We begin to manoeuvre. With his smaller, lighter aircraft – a Camel – he can make tighter circles than I with my heavy Fokker D VII, but I stay behind him. He tries to shake me and starts a loop from barely 100 metres altitude.

Ernst Udet of *Jasta* 4 poses before his most famous D VII in the only clear photograph of this enigmatic machine known to the authors. Naturally, Udet himself obscures much of the machine except for the intriguing wing stripes and the legend *Du doch nicht!!* – loosely translated as 'Certainly not you!!' – on the elevators. A white chevron was added to the dark tailplane, and two black/white streamers were affixed to the elevators. The diagonal striping on the top wing was certainly inspired by Udet's experiences with the black/white striped Dr I of Kirschstein, thus many enthusiasts feel these stripes were black and white instead of the red and white previously favoured. This was probably the first D VII flown by Udet, and there is no primary evidence that he was yet using the red colour scheme so associated with his later aircraft – the tailplane, and nose, may in fact have been *Jasta* 4 black. The finish on the wings would seem to indicate this was an OAW D VII, yet there is also some evidence it may have been Fokker-built. Many questions remain concerning the actual coloration of this popular D VII *(via VanWyngarden)*

I follow on his heels, and at the apex I flash on underneath him. My turning radius is larger than his, and I feel a slight blow, and when I look down again I see him creeping laboriously from the wreckage of his aircraft. German soldiers are picking him up, but I don't know what happened. The only thing I can imagine is that I must have rammed him as I flew past. This was my third fight this day.

'Three days later I visit him in the hospital at Foucaucourt. As a return favour for his leaflets, I bring him a box of cigars made from beech leaves. My surmise was correct. At the apex of the loop, my undercarriage rammed his upper wing, which cracked out beyond the struts. "I wasn't prepared for this kind of clinch fighting", he said jokingly. He is a nice fellow, a student from Ontario.

'Fifteen years later, at a flying meet in Los Angeles, I hear from him again. Roscoe Turner brings me a leaflet while on his non-stop cross-continent flight. It has a black-red-yellow border, having supposedly been sent by German deserters, addressed to the soldiers in the trenches. It is the last of his supply, and he forgot to throw it at me in 1918!'

The pilot was Lt R E Taylor of No 54 Sqn on a special mission – to drop propaganda leaflets to German soldiers in the battle front, as well as to drop bombs. He had last been seen by his comrades at 1930 hrs.

Udet's 60th victory – an SE 5a – was apparently scored in a fight with No 24 Sqn, and in particular its patrol leader, Capt T F Hazell DSO DFC (43 victories). Hazell had attacked a balloon which erupted in flames, but he was in turn attacked by several Fokkers, most prominent among them a 'red enemy aircraft'. Udet chased Hazell back across the lines at low level, both fighters zooming over telegraph poles, trees and around the church tower at Maricourt. The No 24 Sqn report simply states 'Capt Hazell was then seen home by the enemy aircraft, who shot his tank, longerons and propeller to pieces'. Hazell narrowly escaped, but Udet still received a confirmed claim.

The other SE 5as chased Udet off and only just failed to bring him down. Adding to his worries, his phosphorus ammunition began to ignite due to the midday heat. Udet

The irrepressible Ernst Udet was described by a contemporary as a 'short, restless, wiry, ebullient and unusually humorous, often extremely witty, flying leutnant who had been honoured with the *Pour lé Merite'*. The skilled Udet and the BMW-engined D VII were a perfect match, and his final score of 62 would make him the top surviving German ace of the war. Indeed, his tally was only surpassed by Manfred von Richthofen *(via VanWyngarden)*

rapidly fired his guns to get rid of the bullets. Over his shoulder he saw an SE 5a break away, the pilot probably thinking this D VII had unique rear-firing guns due to the white trails left by the ammunition.

Udet's last two victories, Nos 61 and 62, were achieved in his red D VII (F) 4253/18 on 26 September – both were bombers, called 'DH 12s' (sic) in his report, but probably DH 9As. There appears to have been some dispute over these with pilots of *Jasta* 77b, but history has recorded Udet with 62 kills – the second highest scoring fighter ace of Germany in World War 1, and the highest surviving ace. However, in the action of 26 September he was slightly wounded, which put him out of the war for awhile and ended his victory streak.

Between the wars Udet was something of an adventurer, flying whenever and wherever he could, and in America he became a favourite at airshows and races. He also flew aeroplanes in films and as a test pilot. Prior to World War 2, he was persuaded to join the Nazi Party and the Luftwaffe. He rose to the rank of generaloberst, but he was not suited to the political in-fighting, especially against his old commander, Hermann Göring, and others in the Nazi heirarchy. Neither was he temperamentally suited for the intense pressures of his position as Technical Bureau Chief of the RLM (*Reichsluftfahrtministerium*). Unable to cope, he committed suicide in Berlin on 17 November 1941.

Whilst Udet was acting leader of JG I, the black-nosed Fokkers of *Jasta* 4 were led by Ltn Egon Koepsch, a pilot easily recognisable due to his dueling scar. Born on 27 October 1890, he joined *Jasta* 4 on 2 October 1917, following the usual introduction to war flying with a two-seater unit – *Flieger Abteilung* 256. By early 1918 Koepsch had only achieved two victories, yet his acting leadership of the *Jasta* had proved successful, and by war's end he had scored nine kills, seven with the D VII.

Included in these were victories over two British SE 5a aces, namely Capt K W Junor MC (eight victories with No 56 Sqn) on 23 April and Capt John E Doyle DFC (nine victories with No 60 Sqn) on 5 September. In the 1930s Doyle was to write several articles for aviation magazines, and in one of these he described how he was shot down on this day. No 60 Sqn was escorting DH 4 bombers, and being above and behind them, Doyle was in a good place to attack five Fokkers he saw climbing up under the 'fours' after the raid. He recorded;

'I was ideally placed but I decided I must not be in too great a hurry. I must wait until they were nibbling at the bait with their attention thus fully occupied. So I closed my radiator shutter and rocked my machine slowly to attract the attention of my patrol. I wound my tail-trim forward and held the bus up with the stick while I watched the Fokkers' progress with interest. The way they could overhaul empty "Fours" was an education. Then I saw some tracer leave the leading Fokker. It was a long-range shot, but I knew I could not further delay matters. And at that very moment a red Very light curved into the sky from one of the bombers. This was clearly a summons, but hoped it would not cause the Huns to look round.'

Doyle and another pilot dived, but the other SE 5as, for some odd reason, did not. The two British pilots attacked. Doyle saw his fire hit what he felt was the leader, who put his Fokker into a flick turn and dived. He then went after another;

The nine-victory ace Ltn d R Egon Koepsch of *Jasta* 4 – complete with riding crop and dueling scar – sits on the wheel of his BMW-engined Fokker at Metz airfield in August 1918. This machine displayed the black nose, struts and wheel covers of this *Staffel*. Like many other *Jasta* 4 D VIIs, it also had the fuselage longerons marked with black borders, which were often further edged in white – although the white seen here is of a thin and translucent nature. Four-colour printed fabric covered the entire aircraft *(via VanWyngarden)*

'I turned south and was diving after my man. There were two more Fokkers about but, thought I, they will be well marked. I got in another burst and held it while I tried to close up, but the only result was that my man went into a still steeper dive, always flying straight, so I knew I had got him.

'But the laugh was on me also, for a burst of close-range stuff crashed into my SE at that moment. A bullet cracked past just clear of the cockpit, a second went through the instrument panel into the tank and the third struck my head just behind the ear and cut the buckle of my chin-strap, which fell slowly down. Two more cracks and then a terrific concussion. I was pressed against the side of the cockpit, unable to move, while the aeroplane fell headlong, turning on its axis as it did so. Still I was pinned against the side. Petrol was pouring on to me and I managed to depress the switch.'

Doyle was at a loss as to why he was spinning down. Looking down, he noticed that his right flying boot was folded back, but the foot was still on the rudder stirrup. Grabbing the useless limb, he pulled it away from the rudder bar, and with his left leg righted the machine. Looking back he saw two Fokkers still behind him;

'I surmised they were not solicitous for my welfare. I flattened out and hurriedly made a landing of sorts in what appeared to be a park. When the SE had stopped bouncing and come to rest I threw off my seat belt and stood on the seat. A burst of lead from a diving Fokker spattered around me, but I was not hit. When this had stopped I jumped to the ground, tried to take a step and, of course, fell. There was another long burst of firing from above and I lay without moving. Bullets seemed to be smacking into the grass in a circle round my body, but again I was not hit.'

Two German soldiers then appeared and Doyle hobbled over to them. Not long afterward a German pilot came up, Doyle assuming him to be one of the two Fokker pilots, and there followed what appeared to be a fierce altercation between the pilot and a crowd of other soldiers. In due course Doyle gathered that the pilot (probably Koepsch) was enraged because his close friend Joachim von Winterfeld had just been shot down and killed, and this was why he had strafed the SE 5a. Gangrene later set in on Doyle's damaged leg and it was amputated in a German hospital.

On 20 October Koepsch moved briefly to *Jasta* 11, but returned to *Jasta* 4 on 4 November to again take temporary command after Udet's wounding. He survived the war and died on 26 November 1976.

Another 1918 Fokker ace with *Jasta* 4 was Ltn Heinrich Maushake, who had been born in 1894. He, like Koepsch, had joined the unit in late 1917 – 20 November – and survived the war, gaining six official victories with two more unconfirmed. He too had a spell as acting commander in

A variety of styles of flying kit and Heinecke parachute harnesses are in evidence in this clutch of *Jasta* 4 pilots grouped around one of their black-nosed Fokkers at Escaufort airfield on 5 September 1918. From left, with victories noted, are Ltn d R Richard Kraut (one), Ltn d R Robert Hildebrandt (one), Flieger Rohde, Ltn Joachim von Winterfeld (two, killed 5 September), Ltn d R Egon Koepsch (nine, acting *staffelführer* in Udet's absence), Ltn d R Heinrich Maushake on the wing (six), Ltn Heinz Graf von Gluszewski (two), and Ltn d R Julius Bender *(via N W O'Connor)*

October 1918 whilst Udet was in hospital and Koepsch was acting commander of *Jasta* 11. However, on 3 November Maushake was shot down by an American SPAD (apparently from the 103rd Aero Squadron) and wounded, which is why Koepsch returned to take command on the 4th. Despite Maushake's wound, he survived to a ripe old age of 87, dying on 31 August 1981.

The final *Jasta* 4 D VII ace was Ltn Heinrich Drekmann, born in Harburg, on the Elbe, on 5 April 1896. Known as 'Heinz', his first fighter unit had been *Jasta* 26, with whom he gained his first victory – an FE 2d – on 17 August 1917. Less than two weeks later he was reassigned to *Jasta* 4 of the 'Richthofen Circus', but it took him until the following May to gain victory number two, presumably in a triplane.

As with so many others, Drekmann really began to score once he obtained a D VII. He got four kills in June, including a balloon, then a further five in July. It will be remembered that Udet gave him the second BMW-engined D VII the unit received. However, shortly after gaining his 11th victory on 30 July he was shot down in flames and killed at 1835 hrs over Grand Rozoy, probably downed by two pilots of SPA75, Sous-Lt Bamberger and Lt de la Poeze.

JASTA 6

When the D VII began to arrive at *Jasta* 6, its *Staffelführer* was Ltn Johann Janzen. The unit's aircraft were soon decorated with the famous black/white zebra stripes of this *Staffel* on their tailplanes and noses, the *Jasta* making its first war flight completely equipped with the D VII on 19 May. The next day Janzen shot down a Sopwith Dolphin of No 23 Sqn for his eighth victory.

A west Prussian, Janzen was born on 21 May 1896 in Fronza, near Marienwerder. At first a cavalryman, he was commissioned in February 1916 and shortly thereafter transferred to aviation. Flying two-seat bombers with KG 2, he became a fighter pilot with *Jasta* 23 in November 1916, gaining his first kill with this unit the following 25 February. Janzen's next success came on 30 November 1917, by which time he had been posted to *Jasta* 6 on 16 October. On 28 March 1918 he took command of *Jasta* 4, but returned to command *Jasta* 6 on 3 May following Reinhard's promotion to lead JG I. By 7 June Janzen had scored perhaps six D VII victories, which brought his overall score to 13. However, two days later his interrupter gear malfunctioned as he was firing on a French SPAD, smashing his propeller, and he came down in Allied lines to be taken prisoner.

Janzen survived his six months of captivity and in January 1920 joined the *Flieger Staffel* of the Reichswehr at Interberg, where he served until it was disbanded in May. Janzen passed away in the 1980s.

Janzen's place was taken by Ltn Hans Kirschstein, another successful *jagdflieger* with *Jasta* 6 who had achieved a total of 24 victories since 18 March 1918. Despite his success, he was only in temporary command, although this lasted until his death on 16 July. Born in Koblenz on 5 August 1896, Kirschstein initially saw active duty with a sapper outfit (3.*Pionier-Bataillon von Rauch*) in Poland, then served in Galicia, where he contracted malaria which forced his return to the homeland. Although he returned to the front later in the year, Kirschstein transferred to the flying service in May 1917.

He flew two-seaters with Fl. Abt.19, and with this unit undertook a bombing raid on Dover, and also flew several ground attack missions over Flanders, often against tanks. After service with two other two-seater units, his aggression finally got him posted to *Jastaschule* Nr 1 and then to *Jasta* 6 on 13 March. It then took him just five days to gain his first combat victory.

By mid-May Kirschstein had 13 victories against the British, then, with the D VII having arrived, gained a further 14 kills against the French. His D VII, like his previous Dr I, was painted in a 'dazzle' pattern of diagonal black and white stripes to put a pursuing foe off his aim. Although Kirschstein had scored victory No 20 on 3 June – in fact double victories this date against two Bréguet XIVs, followed by three more on the 5th – his *Pour le Mérite* was not awarded until the 24th, the day he gained his 27th success.

Following his leave after his 'Blue Max' award, during which time he had also attended aircraft trials in Germany, Kirschstein returned to *Jasta* 6, but a tragic and useless accident ended his life. He had flown a new machine back to an aviation park for adjustment. Richard Wenzl wrote what happened next;

'So that he could get back right away, a very new comrade went with him, flying the Hannover (a two-seater used as a *Staffel* hack – author). In Fismes, Kirschstein, who couldn't wait to get going, climbed in behind the novice pilot. Markgraf, who had little experience of flying the Hannover, over-controlled the machine. They crashed from an altitude of 50 metres and both died soon afterwards.

'Kirschstein's death hit us hard. Every one of us had a place in his heart for this magnificent and extremely dear man. In him the ranks of combat aviation had lost one of the best disciples of the old school, one who would have been appointed to follow in von Richthofen's footsteps.'

Paul Wenzel (not to be confused with Richard Wenzl) now took temporary command of *Jasta* 6. A little older than most, he was born at Seemuhl on 24 January 1887, so was 30 years of age. He had been in the infantry when war started, only transferring to aviation in 1916. After flying two-seaters he moved to *Jasta* 41 in late 1917, and then to *Jasta* 6 in February 1918. Wenzel had scored four kills by the time the D VII arrived, and by 9 August had raised this to nine. A severe wound two days later ended his flying. This was a combat between *Jasta* 6 and No 209 Sqn RAF in which another pilot, Ltn Bodo von der Wense was killed. Richard Wenzl wrote;

'To my horror, Wense simply flew right at the Englishmen and away from us. By the time he realised his mistake they were all over him. The "pennant man" was right on his tail and shot (text continues on page 47)

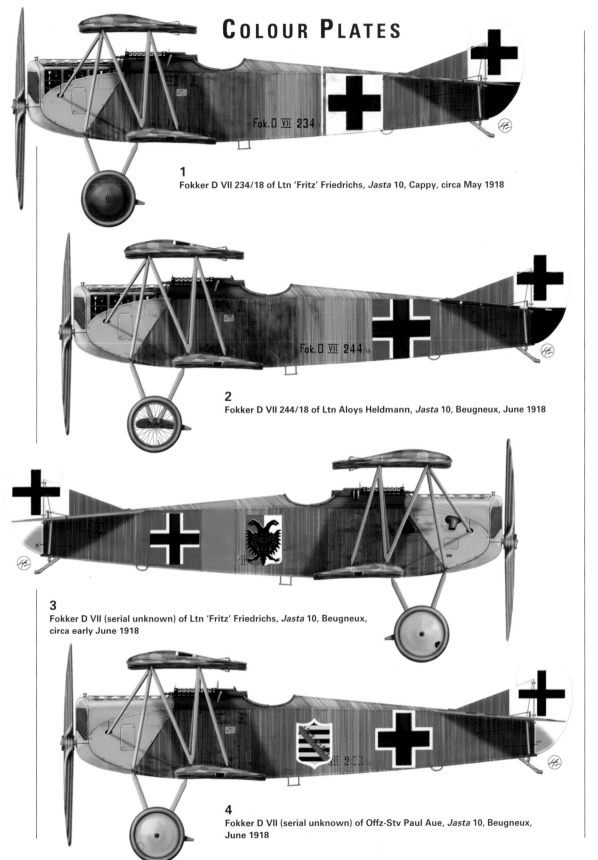

1
Fokker D VII 234/18 of Ltn 'Fritz' Friedrichs, *Jasta* 10, Cappy, circa May 1918

2
Fokker D VII 244/18 of Ltn Aloys Heldmann, *Jasta* 10, Beugneux, June 1918

3
Fokker D VII (serial unknown) of Ltn 'Fritz' Friedrichs, *Jasta* 10, Beugneux, circa early June 1918

4
Fokker D VII (serial unknown) of Offz-Stv Paul Aue, *Jasta* 10, Beugneux, June 1918

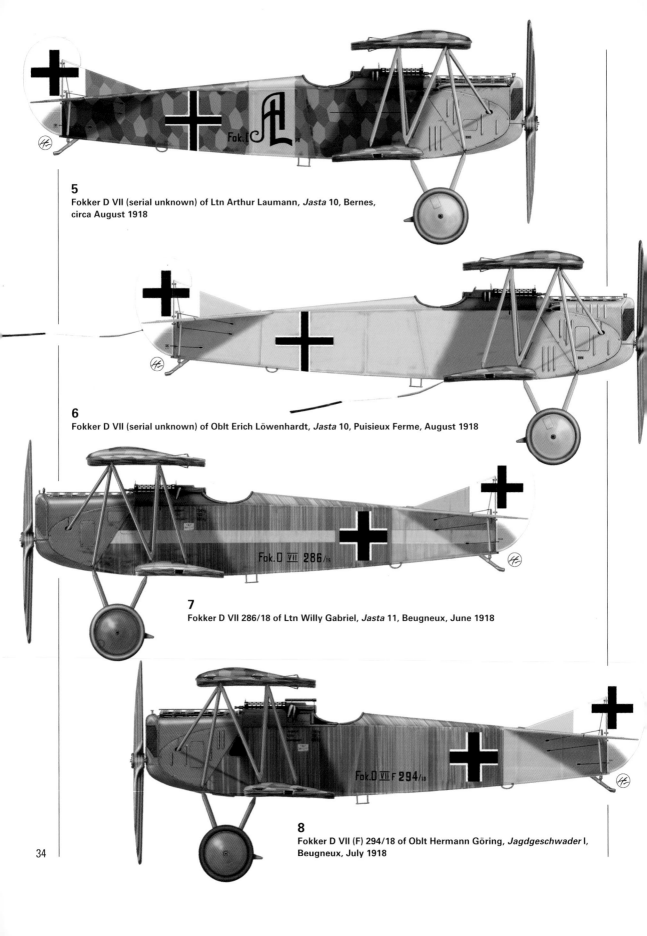

5
Fokker D VII (serial unknown) of Ltn Arthur Laumann, *Jasta* 10, Bernes,
circa August 1918

6
Fokker D VII (serial unknown) of Oblt Erich Löwenhardt, *Jasta* 10, Puisieux Ferme, August 1918

7
Fokker D VII 286/18 of Ltn Willy Gabriel, *Jasta* 11, Beugneux, June 1918

8
Fokker D VII (F) 294/18 of Oblt Hermann Göring, *Jagdgeschwader* I,
Beugneux, July 1918

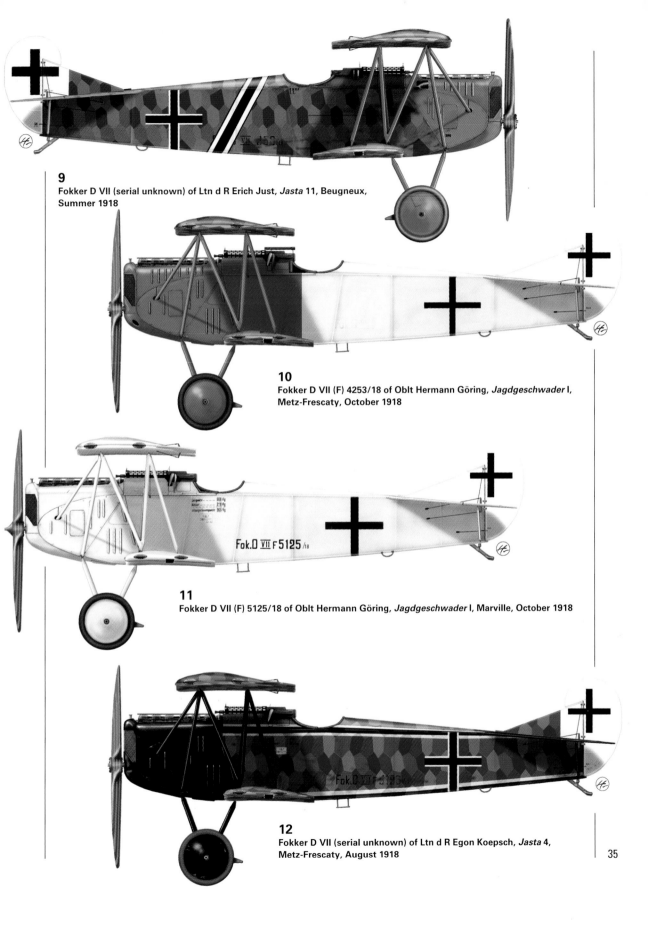

9
Fokker D VII (serial unknown) of Ltn d R Erich Just, *Jasta* 11, Beugneux,
Summer 1918

10
Fokker D VII (F) 4253/18 of Oblt Hermann Göring, *Jagdgeschwader* I,
Metz-Frescaty, October 1918

11
Fokker D VII (F) 5125/18 of Oblt Hermann Göring, *Jagdgeschwader* I, Marville, October 1918

12
Fokker D VII (serial unknown) of Ltn d R Egon Koepsch, *Jasta* 4,
Metz-Frescaty, August 1918

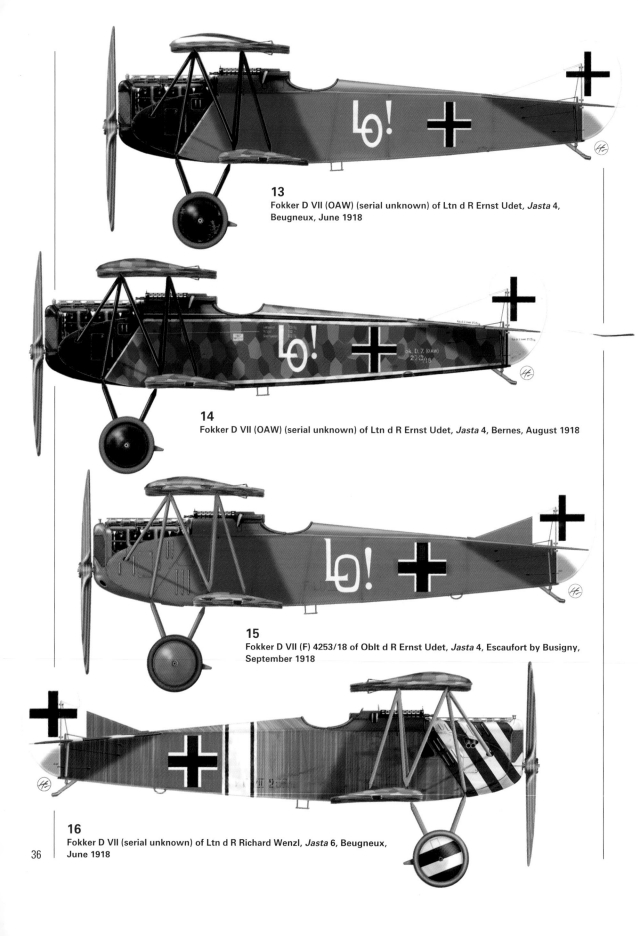

13
Fokker D VII (OAW) (serial unknown) of Ltn d R Ernst Udet, *Jasta* 4,
Beugneux, June 1918

14
Fokker D VII (OAW) (serial unknown) of Ltn d R Ernst Udet, *Jasta* 4, Bernes, August 1918

15
Fokker D VII (F) 4253/18 of Oblt d R Ernst Udet, *Jasta* 4, Escaufort by Busigny,
September 1918

16
Fokker D VII (serial unknown) of Ltn d R Richard Wenzl, *Jasta* 6, Beugneux,
June 1918

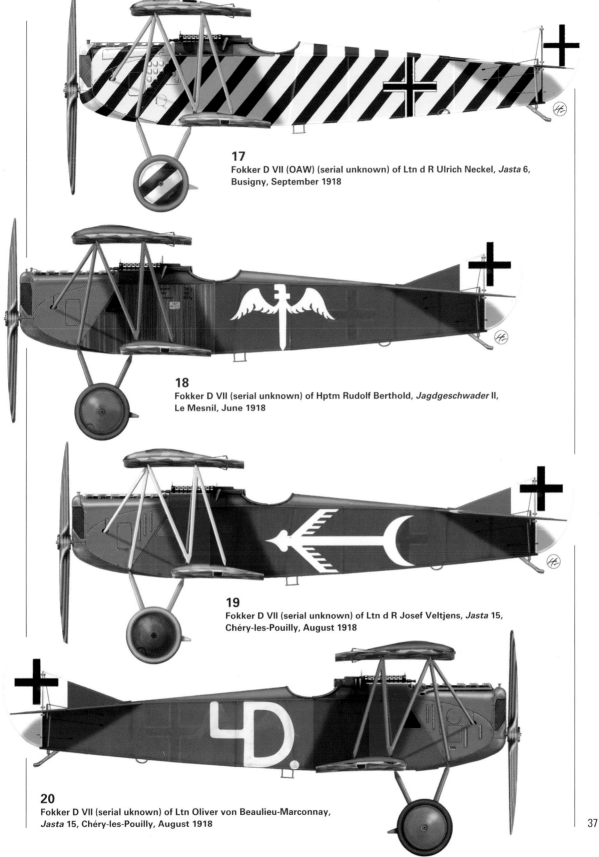

17
Fokker D VII (OAW) (serial unknown) of Ltn d R Ulrich Neckel, *Jasta* 6,
Busigny, September 1918

18
Fokker D VII (serial unknown) of Hptm Rudolf Berthold, *Jagdgeschwader* II,
Le Mesnil, June 1918

19
Fokker D VII (serial unknown) of Ltn d R Josef Veltjens, *Jasta* 15,
Chéry-les-Pouilly, August 1918

20
Fokker D VII (serial uknown) of Ltn Oliver von Beaulieu-Marconnay,
Jasta 15, Chéry-les-Pouilly, August 1918

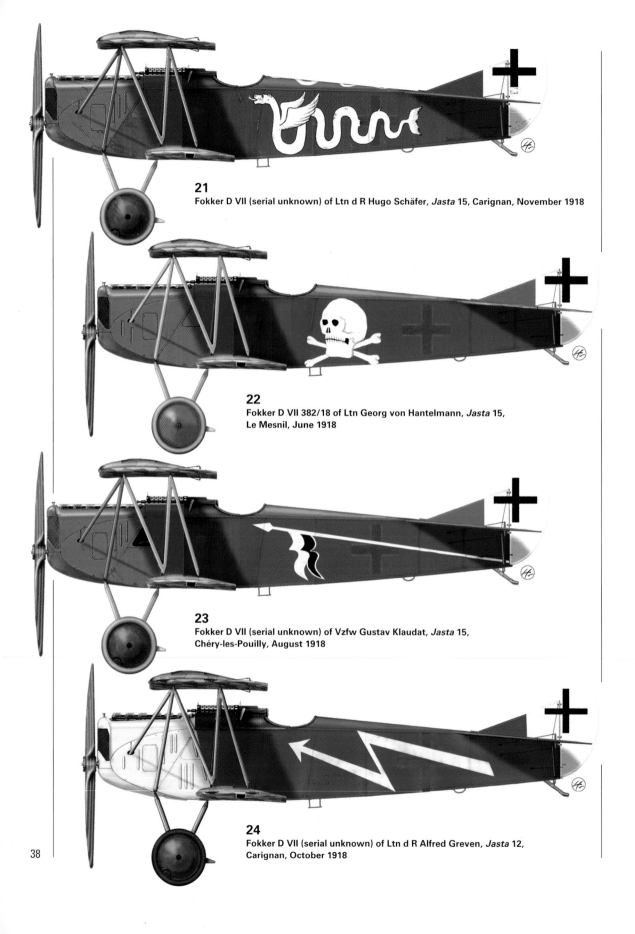

21
Fokker D VII (serial unknown) of Ltn d R Hugo Schäfer, *Jasta* 15, Carignan, November 1918

22
Fokker D VII 382/18 of Ltn Georg von Hantelmann, *Jasta* 15,
Le Mesnil, June 1918

23
Fokker D VII (serial unknown) of Vzfw Gustav Klaudat, *Jasta* 15,
Chéry-les-Pouilly, August 1918

24
Fokker D VII (serial unknown) of Ltn d R Alfred Greven, *Jasta* 12,
Carignan, October 1918

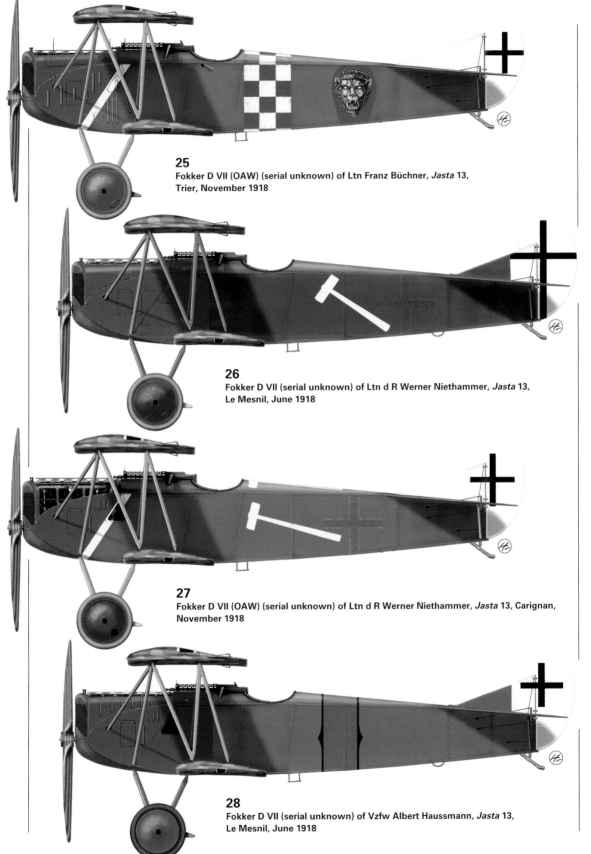

25
Fokker D VII (OAW) (serial unknown) of Ltn Franz Büchner, *Jasta* 13,
Trier, November 1918

26
Fokker D VII (serial unknown) of Ltn d R Werner Niethammer, *Jasta* 13,
Le Mesnil, June 1918

27
Fokker D VII (OAW) (serial unknown) of Ltn d R Werner Niethammer, *Jasta* 13, Carignan,
November 1918

28
Fokker D VII (serial unknown) of Vzfw Albert Haussmann, *Jasta* 13,
Le Mesnil, June 1918

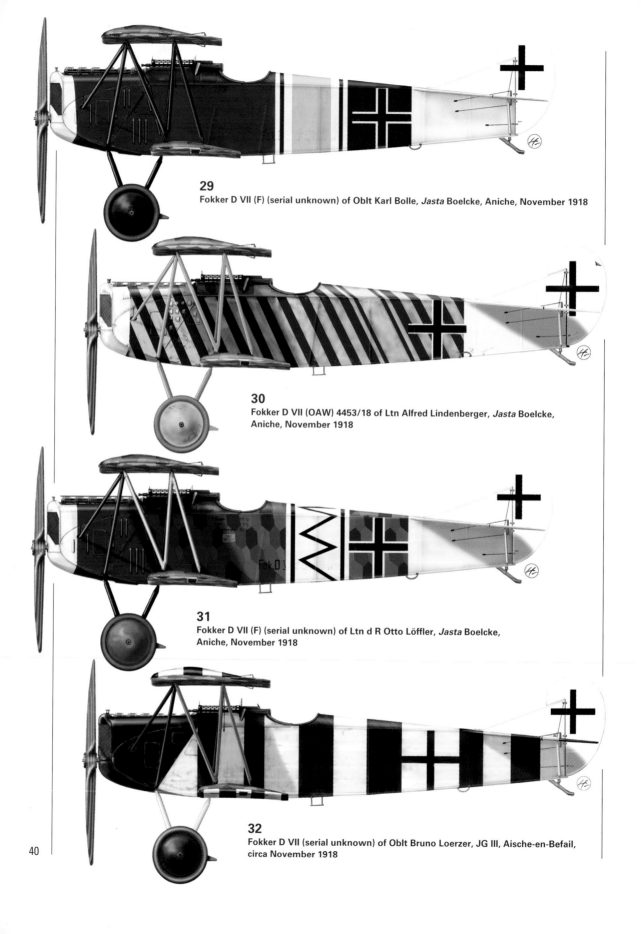

29
Fokker D VII (F) (serial unknown) of Oblt Karl Bolle, *Jasta* Boelcke, Aniche, November 1918

30
Fokker D VII (OAW) 4453/18 of Ltn Alfred Lindenberger, *Jasta* Boelcke, Aniche, November 1918

31
Fokker D VII (F) (serial unknown) of Ltn d R Otto Löffler, *Jasta* Boelcke, Aniche, November 1918

32
Fokker D VII (serial unknown) of Oblt Bruno Loerzer, JG III, Aische-en-Befail, circa November 1918

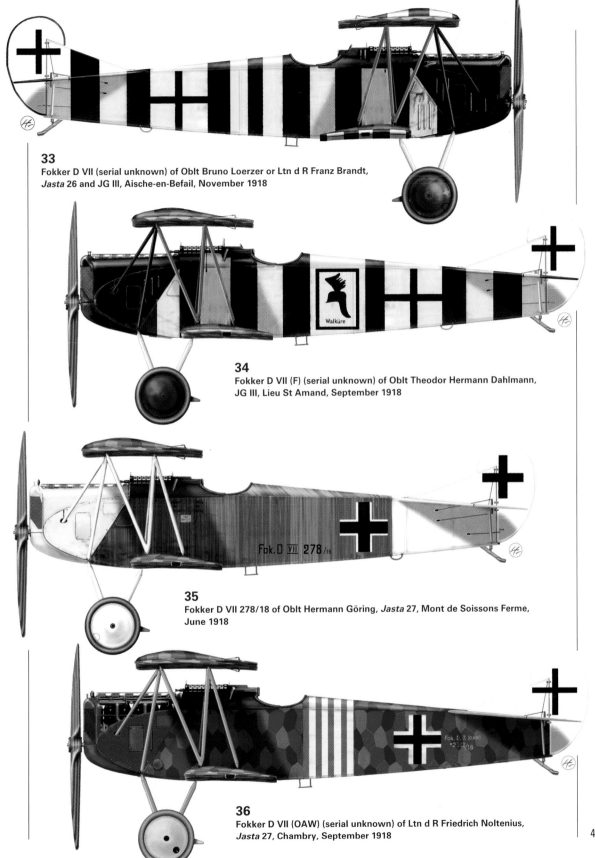

33
Fokker D VII (serial unknown) of Oblt Bruno Loerzer or Ltn d R Franz Brandt,
Jasta 26 and JG III, Aische-en-Befail, November 1918

34
Fokker D VII (F) (serial unknown) of Oblt Theodor Hermann Dahlmann,
JG III, Lieu St Amand, September 1918

35
Fokker D VII 278/18 of Oblt Hermann Göring, *Jasta* 27, Mont de Soissons Ferme,
June 1918

36
Fokker D VII (OAW) (serial unknown) of Ltn d R Friedrich Noltenius,
Jasta 27, Chambry, September 1918

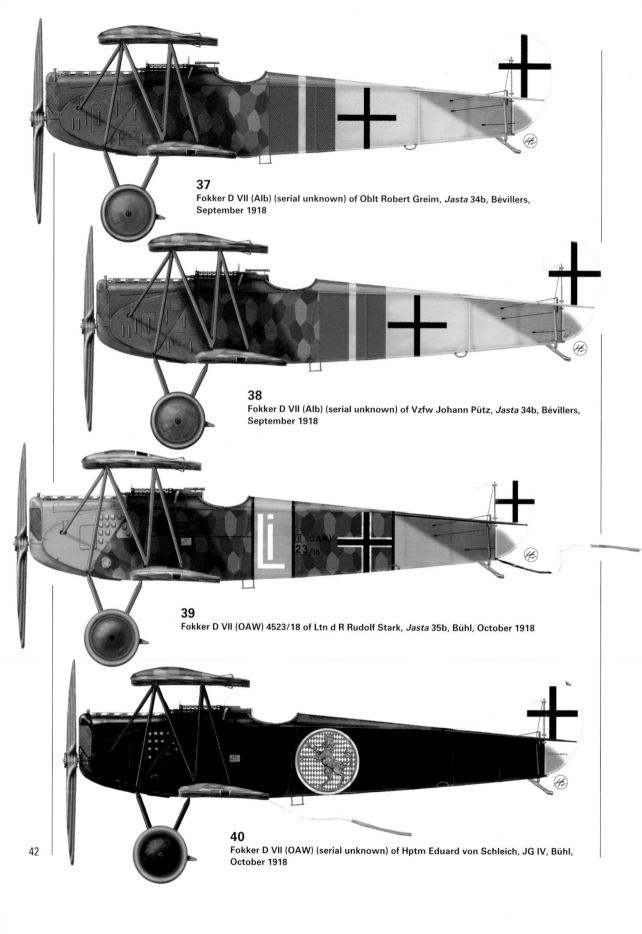

37
Fokker D VII (Alb) (serial unknown) of Oblt Robert Greim, *Jasta* 34b, Bévillers,
September 1918

38
Fokker D VII (Alb) (serial unknown) of Vzfw Johann Pütz, *Jasta* 34b, Bévillers,
September 1918

39
Fokker D VII (OAW) 4523/18 of Ltn d R Rudolf Stark, *Jasta* 35b, Bühl, October 1918

40
Fokker D VII (OAW) (serial unknown) of Hptm Eduard von Schleich, JG IV, Bühl,
October 1918

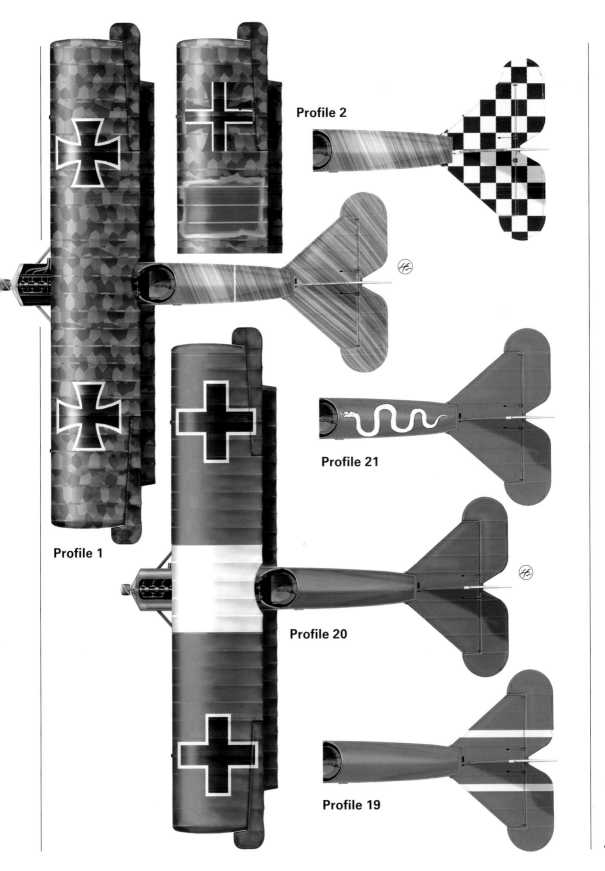

Profile 2

Profile 21

Profile 1

Profile 20

Profile 19

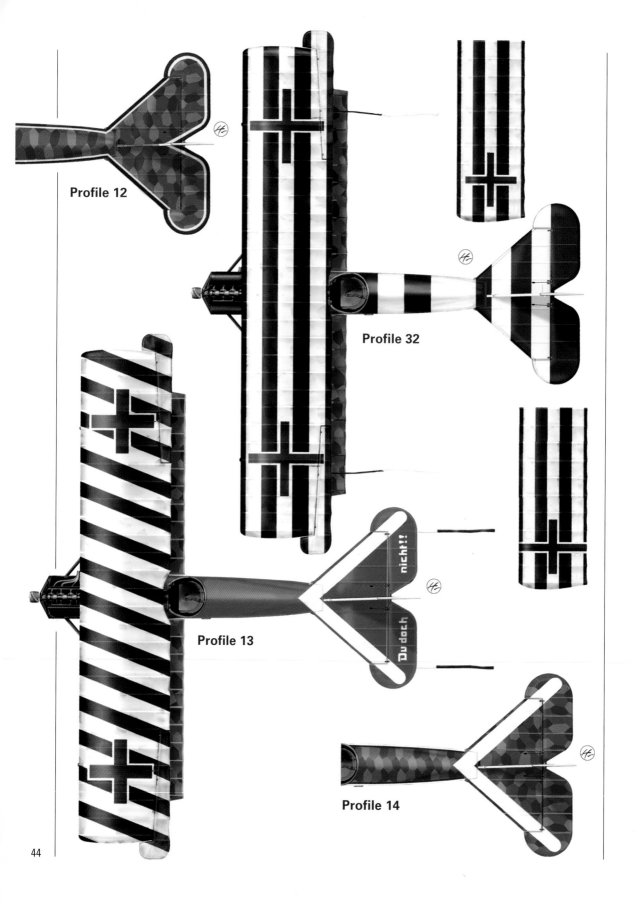

Profile 12

Profile 32

Profile 13

Du doch nicht!!

Profile 14

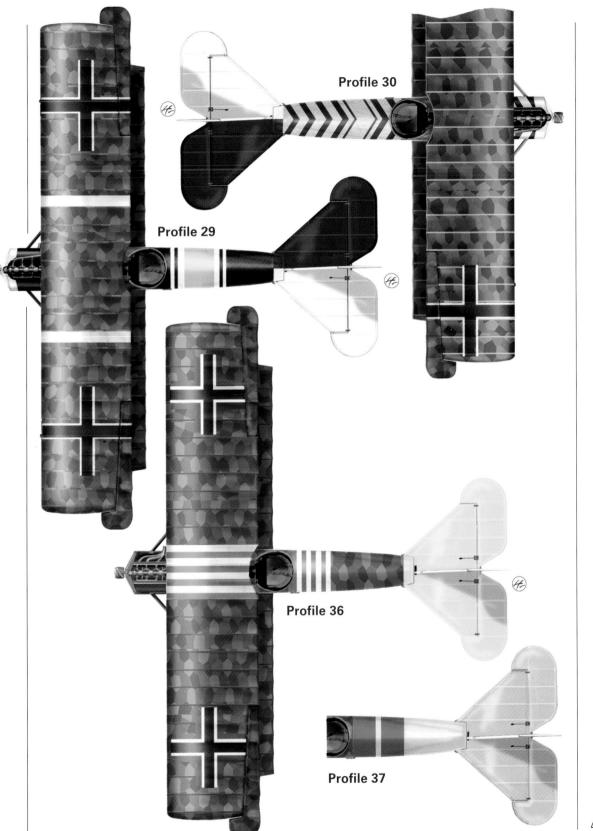

Profile 30

Profile 29

Profile 36

Profile 37

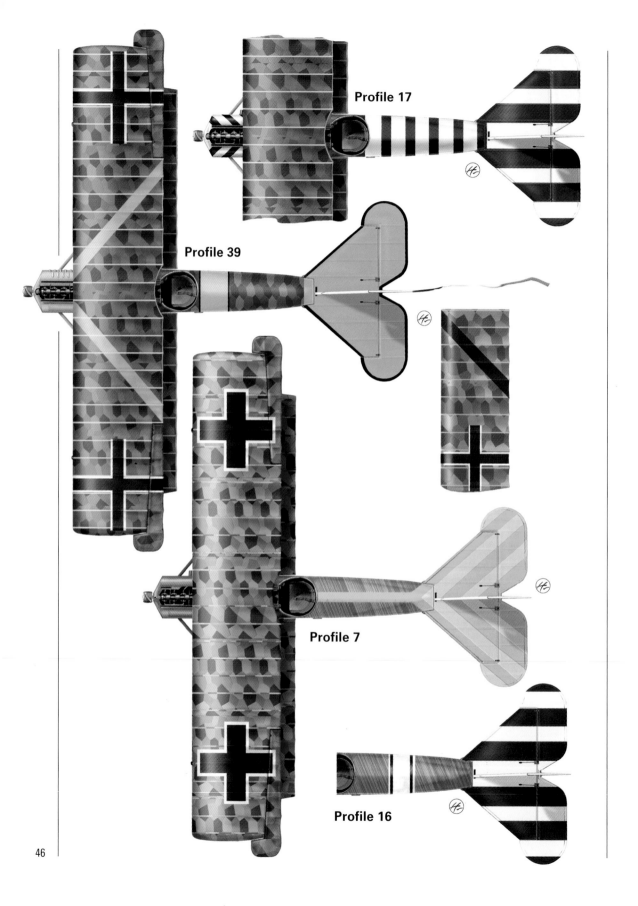

Profile 17

Profile 39

Profile 7

Profile 16

Ltn Paul Wenzel of *Jasta* 6 (not to be confused with fellow *Staffel* pilot Richard Wenzl, seen below) scored ten kills and served as acting CO from 19 July 1918 until he was badly wounded on 11 August. His final six victories were probably scored on the D VII *(HAC/UTD)*

Jasta 6's 12-kill ace Richard Wenzl

An early-production Fokker-built D VII of *Jasta* 6 beautifully displays the unit's black/white stripes on nose, tail and wheels, and also Richard Wenzl's personal emblem of a fuselage band in the proportions of the iron cross ribbon, but with colours reversed. This may well be Wenzl's first D VII, which he received on 18 May – the national insignia shows signs of conversion from a previous format. Note the style of exhaust exit and the abundantly louvred cowling panel *(via VanWyngarden)*

him down as I tried to intervene. Then there was a hot battle as all the single-seaters – easily 25 of them – came down at us. The British "pennant man" came down and fired at me. I can still see his big red cowling and the two red pennants on his wing struts.'

Wenzl was slightly wounded in a long battle with the 'pennant man', but not seriously enough to curtail his flying. However, No 209 Sqn had knocked out Wense and Paul Wenzel, Capt John K Summers MC (the flight leader and 'pennant man') claiming one of the Fokkers, while Lt Kenneth M Walker claimed the other. The next day, as already stated, both Summers and Walker were brought down by Lothar von Richthofen, Walker being killed.

Paul Wenzel served in the Luftwaffe in World War 2, and was a survivor in the Heinkel He 111 crash which killed World War 2 ace Werner Mölders in November 1941 – they were on their way to Udet's funeral in Berlin. Wenzel died in Germany on 30 January 1964, aged 77.

Richard Wenzl, meanwhile, had moved from *Jasta* 11 to *Jasta* 6 in May 1918, and was now flying the D VII. His modest score began to increase until by war's end he had achieved a total of 12 kills, the last going down on 5 November. He wrote of the day he received his D VII at *Jasta* 6;

'On 18 May I too got my new Fokker D VII and had it arranged the way I wanted it. This biplane was again equipped with the 160-hp Mercedes engine. We were astounded at what Fokker had been able to wring out of the long-outdated engine. The new biplane was not as manoeuvrable as our triplanes, but it was somewhat speedier. It was a little slow climbing at low altitude, but it climbed better at high altitude, as we had the high-compression engines which were designed for high altitude.

'On the 19th we made our first flight together as a *Staffel* with the D VII. Right away we pounced on a squadron of bombers, but as we did so, we were attacked from above by SE 5s. Although I was still unfamiliar with my D VII, I made a smooth turn over my opponent, got him in front of me and just waited for my bursts of fire to take effect. He was already seeking lower altitudes – and far this side of the lines – when there was a "bang" in my machine and I heard the merry chatter of a machine-gun behind me. But that just couldn't be possible, for I had been paying close attention, and the only machine behind me was a D VII. I was forced to make a quick turn as the bullets were becoming very disconcerting to me.

'It turned out that one of my *Staffel* comrades, mistaking me for a Tommy, had merrily turned his machine-guns on me. It was a forgivable mistake because the D VII did bear a certain similarity to the SE 5. And so, once again, another opponent had slipped away from me.'

On leave from the first week in September, Wenzl returned at the start of October. He discovered that the *Geschwader* was about to move to

Ltn d R Ulrich Neckel became the last *Staffelführer* of *Jasta* 6 on 1 September 1918, having already achieved 24 victories in various JG II units. As CO of *Jagdstaffel* 6, he had the unit's black/white identity stripes extended to the entire fuselage of his various D VIIs, including this OAW-built example guarded by his teddy bear mascot – a popular touch. Note the light-coloured rib tapes on the four-colour fabric on the top wing *(via VanWyngarden)*

A fine view of the D VII (OAW) flown by Ulrich Neckel as leader of *Jasta* 6. The oblique striping on the fuselage undoubtedly helped to identify the *Staffelführer* in the air, but it was also believed to throw off the aim of a pursuing pilot by optical illusion. Neckel flew perhaps two other D VIIs similarly marked. Along with Degelow of *Jasta* 40, Neckel would become one of the last two aviation recipients of the 'Blue Max' *(via VanWyngarden)*

Metz due to the American offensive, although JG II had 'already skimmed off the cream – the Americans had absolutely no experience in air combat, and they suffered terrible losses'. Wenzl also noted that everyone now had the BMW-engined D VII, which more than proved itself in the coming days. Wenzl scored a double over two SPADs on 3 November for his 10th and 11th kills. He recorded;

'There was very little going on at the front. Far behind the lines, over Bois de la Côte Lemont, west of Sivry on the Meuse, three SPADs were wheeling. Since we were higher, I tried to get close and came to within 300 metres before they turned off. As we were flying back to the lines, they came after us. Now we quickly throttled back so that they could catch up, then we about-turned!

'The three SPADs had turned into six SPADs. I got one of the upper ones to bite at 20 metres. Right after my first burst, during which he gamely held still, he broke off, heading straight down. I took it to be a trick and immediately attached myself to the next one, who had noticed me from below. Of course, like a real amateur, he immediately turned, so that I was sitting right behind him.

'After about 100 rounds he started to smoke, and attempted to escape below. Meanwhile, I look around and happened to notice – oh, joy – that my first opponent was still falling like a rock. He went in just east of Nantillois and disintegrated into atoms.

'My second opponent, whom I had understandably neglected for a moment, had righted his machine and was in a flat glide with his engine smoking badly. He didn't even notice that I had once again positioned myself behind him, and no doubt he felt himself to be quite safe under the protection of his comrades flying nearby.

'He got shot down anyway and went rushing down into the depths, just like his predecessor. In order to see the moment of impact for myself, I went down after him, to 1400 metres. On the edge of the village of Montfaucon he fell into a type of vegetable garden and there he was incinerated.

'So that had been a splendid double. Now, of course, I got real swell-headed and I wasn't even afraid of the other four SPADs which accompanied me back to the front without seriously attacking me. If they had been Englishmen, I would have been a lost man.'

Richard Wenzl survived the war with the Knight's Cross with Swords of the Royal Hohenzollern House Order (known as 'the Hohenzollern') and the Iron Cross 1st class. Immediately after the war he fought against the communists, and served in Franz von Epp's Freikorps that saw action in Munich in May 1919. Wenzl died in 1957.

It has already been mentioned that Friedrich Noltenius served only briefly in *Jasta* 6, yet he still obtained two victories with the unit. On 6 October he was flying D VII 5056/18 marked with his red/white band on the fuselage. He made his first mark in the *Geschwader* record

book that day by making a carefully planned attack on a French balloon. Four days later Noltenius attacked two SPADs which were escorting a Bréguet, his fire raking one of them which broke up in the air. On 18 October, however, Noltenius was somewhat unfairly reprimanded by his commander, Ltn d R Neckel, for 'deserting' him during a fight with some SPADs, and he transferred to *Staffel* 11.

Ulrich Neckel was in fact the last full commander of *Jasta* 6. He took over on 1 September once it was realised that Paul Wenzel would not be able to return to full duty. Neckel was a 24-victory ace following service with *Jastas* 12, 13 and 19, and he shall be mentioned again in the section on JG II. As far as the *Pour le Mérite* was concerned, things were not so clear cut as in earlier times, and 20 victories was no longer the automatic yard-stick for its award. In fact Neckel did not receive his until 8 November, two days after his 30th victory claim – he was one of the last two aviation recipients of the 'Blue Max'.

Leading *Jasta* 6 in his black and white striped Fokkers, he claimed his last six victories between 15 September and 6 November 1918. His 30th victory was also the final success for JG I, when elements of *Jastas* 6 and 10 tangled with SPADs of the US 28th Aero Squadron – the American unit lost 1Lts Ben Brown (PoW) and Hugh McClung (killed), although the *Geschwader* was credited with three victories.

The American patrol of three SPADs had just downed a two-seater when they were bounced by five Fokkers at low altitude. Brown was pursued by four of the *Geschwader* pilots to a low height, and he later described the engagement;

'I was now so close to the ground that manoeuvring was difficult and I could no longer get away from the stream of tracers. Bullets were coming through the cockpit and I was hit in one finger. The machine crashed and I was unconscious for a while. The German soldiers had pulled me from the wreck and bound up my finger. The four Fokker pilots who had chased me came down to Loupy le Chateau to shake hands with me. Ltn Neckel was their Flight Commander. He told me who he was and then complimented me for getting the biplane. They seemed to be a very sporty lot of pilots.'

Altough he survived the war, Ulrich Neckel contracted tuberculosis some years later and eventually died from this disease while in Italy on 11 May 1928.

JG I completed a move to Metz-Frescaty by 28 September, where this interesting line-up photograph was taken. Second from left is a Fokker-built D VII bearing Ulrich Neckel's fully-striped fuselage markings. While two other machines seen here display *Jasta* 6 markings, this may be a mixed group including aircraft from *Jastas* 4 or 11, or simply some machines in factory finish *(via VanWyngarden)*

A well-turned out group of *Jasta* 6 pilots show off their indispensable walking sticks. At the extreme left is Ltn d R Julius Schmidt, who had scored 15 victories in *Jasta* 3 but was then severely wounded, and apparently did little flying after transferring to *Jasta* 6 on 9 September. Next to him is Ltn d R Neckel, the unit's CO, then Ltn d R Werner Nöldecke (one victory), Ltn Matzdorf (two) in flying togs and Ltn Schliewen *(via VanWyngarden)*

JG II – BERTHOLD'S BLUE BIRDS

The successes of Manfred von Richthofen's JG I throughout the second half of 1917, together with the preparations for the great German Spring Offensive of March 1918, convinced the German High Command of the need for two more *Jagdgeschwadern,* each to be permanently composed of four *Jagdstaffeln.* With this increase in *Geschwadern*, it would be possible to allocate a *Jagdgeschwader* to each of the three attacking armies engaged in the offensive (codenamed Operation *Michael,* and later known as the *'Kaiserschlacht').* Therefore, JG II and JG III were formed, effective from 2 February 1918.

Within months of its formation, JG II had had to be reassigned to less aggressive operations due to problems with its elderly Fokker Dr Is, which were blighted by engine unreliablity caused by poor-quality lubricating oil. By early June 1918 *Jasta* 12, 13 and 19s effectiveness was seriously hampered, and only *Staffel* 15, which had received 15 D VIIs was in combat. Only gradually did the other three units get D VIIs as they became available. In fact *Jasta* 12 had to continue with its Dr Is for some time.

However, on 14 July the *Geschwader* received 20 D VIIs, nine going to *Jasta* 12, three to *Jasta* 13 and eight to *Jasta* 19. The Fokkers of JG II would be painted predominantly blue on their fuselage and tail surfaces, with each *Staffel* identified by differently coloured noses – white for *Jasta* 12, green for 13, red for 15 and yellow for *Jasta* 19. The War Diary noted at this period, 'For the first time since its formation, the *Geschwader* has been equipped with one type of aircraft, and looks forward with anticipation to the offensive which will begin on 15th July'.

This anticipation was fully realised. For instance, in an army communiqué dated 20 September;

'Over the Battlefields between the Maas and Mosel, *Jagdgeschwader* II, under the command of Oblt Freiherr von Boenigk, shot down 81 enemy aircraft between 12 and 18 September, losing only two of their own in battle.'

JAGDGESCHWADER II

JG II was formed around *Jastas* 12, 13, 15 and 19. The initial *Kommandeur* was Hptm Adolf von Tutschek, legendary leader of *Jasta* 12. Like its predecessor, JG II would be a mobile unit. The formation and its leader reported direct to Army HQ AOK (*Armee-Ober-Kommando*). Initially, JG II was assigned to the 7. *Armee.*

Adolf von Tutschek was a celebrated Bavarian fighter ace with 23 victories and the 'Blue Max'. He would also gain three more kills with his new command before falling in combat on 15 March.

The four *Jastas* brought with them a variety of fighters – Albatros D Vas, Pfalz D IIIas and Fokker Dr Is – and with these the *Geschwader* commenced operations. Before the D VIIs arrived, JG II received a few Siemens-Schuckert D III fighters, which had a terrific rate of climb but suffered chronic engine failures. As the Dr I was also forced out of front line duty due to engine problems, the situation deteriorated until *Jasta* 12 and *Jasta* 13 were virtually out of aircraft. Things began to improve with the arrival of a few D VIIs for *Jasta* 15 in mid-June, and as the supply started to increase, the remaining three units started to re-equip as well.

JG II *KOMMANDEURS*

The major change in JG II, of course, was in the leadership following the early loss of von Tutschek. The new *Kommandeur* was the equally legendary Hptm Rudolf Berthold, later labelled the 'Iron Knight'. Berthold was one of the few successful Eindecker pilots from the 1915 era to survive this long, having commanded both *Jastas* 14 and 18. From Ditterswind, near Bamberg, he was born on 24 March 1891, the son of a Franconian forester, and had served with the infantry since 1910.

Learning to fly in 1913, Berthold naturally joined the air service when war came, and apart from wounds and injuries, had not stopped flying since. His wounds, however, had been considerable, and at times he had suffered a broken pelvis, fractured skull, broken nose, broken thigh, smashed upper right arm and several bullet injuries. Indeed, Berthold had been severely wounded in October 1917, and had only now managed to talk his way back into a combat unit, although his most recent arm wounds had not yet healed and were still festering. Like his warlord Kaiser Wilhelm II, Berthold had almost lost the complete use of his right arm. With pieces of bone continually working their way through his flesh, the wound was not healing at all. A more reasonable man would have decided enough was enough – he already had the *Pour le Mérite* and 28 victories.

Berthold, however, was not one to let pain detract him from his grim – even fanatical – determination to lead. He demanded much from his men, but never more than he demanded of himself. Following 21 April, Berthold wrote to his sister;

'Richthofen's killed, daily the comrades fall, the English are numerically superior. I must show the young ones that duty stands above everything else'.

JG II 's formidable and grimly determined *Kommandeur* Hptm Rudolf Berthold scored perhaps his final 12 victories flying the D VII. The famous aircraft seen here bore *Jasta* 15 colours of a red engine cowling and dark blue fuselage (from the cockpit midpoint aft) and tail surfaces. Berthold's famous winged sword emblem was emblazoned on the fuselage in white. An early Fokker-built machine, this D VII still displayed the factory streaked camouflage from the cowling panels aft to the cockpit. The uppersurfaces of both wings were apparently dark blue as well to help distinguish the *Geschwader* commander's aircraft – the centre section of the top wing was seemingly painted white. Note the fuselage cross insignia, still visible through the translucent blue paint *(via VanWyngarden)*

The resolute and aggressive Franconian Rudolf Berthold is seen here in an earlier – and somewhat healthier – period. On 25 April 1916 he crashed his Pfalz E IV, suffering a severe skull injury, and a broken pelvis, thigh and nose. On 20 October 1917 his upper right arm was shattered by machine gun bullets, rendering the limb useless. Berthold duly taught himself to write with his left hand and lobbied hard to be returned to active service. In March 1918 he was given command of JG II, following von Tutschek's death *(via VanWyngarden)*

The 'old Franconian' had always imposed strict discipline on the ground and tight formation flying in the air. Apparently this did not sit well with some of the *Jasta* leaders in JG II, as Berthold wrote in his diary on 25 April;

'I have so many worries and annoyances – I must have three *Staffelführer* removed. It is a hard blow. Instead of teamwork, one finds difficulties. The *Staffelführer* had organised a type of plot in order to over-throw me. I will be ruthlessly hard. The boys should be ashamed of themselves and I can get the "sad brothers" out easier.'

Indeed, the iron-willed Berthold soon did have three new loyal *Jasta* commanders in the *Geschwader*, and despite his injuries was determined to fly again. Berthold wrote;

'28 May 1918. Because the arrival of my new "crate" (a D VII – author) was taking too long, JG I gave me one of the same type. It flies very comfortably. Above all, the controls are so light that I can even handle them with my right arm.'

That same day he took off in his new D VII in front of *Jasta* 15, and shot down a French aircraft over Soissons. The next day came victory No 30 – a SPAD south of Soissons – followed by a Bréguet ten minutes later. By the end of June Berthold's score had reached 37, and two more aircraft fell to him in July.

Some of his other letters from this period (translated by O'Brien Browne) give an evocative picture of the fanatical JG II commander;

'19 June 1918. It's raining today. Thank God, because otherwise it would have been impossible for me to fly with the others. My arm has gotten worse. It is rather swollen and infected underneath the still open wound. I believe the bone splinters are forcibly pushing themselves out because the swollen area is very hard. The pain is incredible. During my air battle yesterday, in which I shot down in flames two English single-seaters, I screamed out loud from the pain. All the swelling came overnight.

'28 June 1918. Yesterday I flew again – which I hadn't done since I shot down my 36th opponent – and I shot down in flames my 37th. My arm is still no good. Since the lower wound has broken open again, the pain has diminished somewhat and the swelling has reduced. Last week was horrible. I screamed from the pain, at times I went into a fit. It appears to have only been a bone splinter. From outside, you could directly follow the path which it wandered. In the end it got stuck in the old, scarred wound, then the fun really started for me. After a few days, as the scar popped open and the pus sprayed out in a high arc, a bit of relief at least came.

'I know that I feel every – even the slightest – pain double and triply, because since being wounded I have not had time to bring my body up to its old capability for resistance. And because I was also otherwise never granted peace, the war, of course, has extremely weakened me. But I must hang in there no matter what it costs. After the war we can slowly bring my old bones back into order again.'

Despite all this pain which most men would have felt, justifiably, warranted a long leave from the front, Berthold fought on. According to the reminiscences of two of his pilots (Paul Strähle and Georg von Hantelmann), he only kept going with the aid of morphine, and his loyal pilots 'made allowances' for his increasingly difficult behaviour. Berthold claimed his 40th victory on 1 July, and then came his final combat days as the Allied Amiens Offensive started in August. Two victories on the 9th were followed by two DH 4 bombers on the 10th, but he collided with the second one and, unable to control his crippled Fokker, especially with his useless right arm, his attempted force-landing ended with a crash into a derelict house.

The resultant further injuries now put him out of the war. In April 1919 this ardent nationalist joined the Freikorps during the civil strife which followed the global fighting, leading some 1200 men in his 'Franconian Farmer's Detachment' – 'Berthold's Iron Band'. His 'Eiserne Schar' took part in the Kapp-Lüttwitz Putsch of March 1920. Berthold was killed by communists on 15 March 1920 in Harburg, on the Elbe, after reportedly agreeing to terms whereby he and his men could evacuate the area without arms, and have these returned outside the town. No sooner did Berthold start to lead his men out than he was attacked, clubbed to the ground and brutally killed. The well-known story that he was strangled with the ribbon of his *Pour le Mérite* is certainly mere propaganda, but typical. On his grave was inscribed 'fighter for Germany's honour, victor in 44 aerial combats, honoured by the enemy – slain by his German brothers'.

Josef Veltjens was given temporary command of the *Geschwader* until the end of August, at which time Oblt Oskar Freiherr von Boenigk arrived from *Jasta* 21 to take over. Von Boenigk came from Silesia, born on 25 August 1893 in Siegersdorf, near Bunzlau. He became an army cadet, aged 11, and was commissioned in March 1912 into a grenadier regiment. Leading a platoon at the start of the war, von Boenigk was wounded in October 1914, and once back in action, was wounded again in 1915. Returning to the front, he then transferred to the air service in late 1915 to become an observer. After pilot training, von Boenigk went to *Jasta* 4 in June 1917, scored seven kills by the autumn and became CO of *Staffel* 21. On 11 August 1918 he claimed his 21st victory (a tally which included seven balloons), and then came the summons to lead JG II.

Flying the D VII as *Geschwader* leader, von Boenigk scored five victories during September 1918 to bring his score to 26. The *Pour le Mérite* came on 25 October – the same date as Franz Büchner (*Jasta* 12) and Arthur Laumann (*Jasta* 10) received their awards.

Von Boenigk also saw action during the post-war revolution and later served in the Luftwaffe during World War 2 as a major-general. Although he retired on 31 May 1943, it is understood he later became a captive of the Russians in May 1945 and died in a prison camp on 30 January 1946.

The last of JG II's three commanders was Oblt Oskar Freiherr von Boenigk with 26 victories. Like the von Richthofen brothers, he was of Silesian nobility and would earn the *Pour le Mérite*. He had led *Jasta* 21 before taking command of *Jagdgeschwader* II *(via VanWyngarden)*

GESCHWADER ACES

Jasta 12

Ltn Hermann Becker served with *Jasta* 12 from May 1917 until war's end, by which time he was its commander. Born on 10 September 1887, he had joined the air service in 1916, flying two-seaters on the Eastern Front as an observer. Following pilot training, Becker served with KG 5 and then with *Schutzstaffel* 11 in France, where he saw action over the Somme and at Verdun.

Commissioned in November 1916, with both classes of the Iron Cross, Becker transferred onto single-seaters and went to *Jasta* 12. He did not get off to a great start, for after downing his first victory on 6 June 1917 he was wounded in a fight with No 60 Sqn ten days later and did not return to the front until the late summer. By the time *Jasta* 12 had become part of JG II Becker had scored 11 victories.

The final OAW-built D VII flown by Ltn d R Alfred Greven of *Jasta* 12 was handed over to the Americans at war's end, and the fuselage is seen here stored at Romorantin, awaiting shipment to the USA. The tyres have been removed, but the aircraft still displays the dark blue and white markings of *Staffel* 12, as well as Greven's personal lightning bolt insignia in white. Greven probably achieved his four victories in D VIIs in the last two months of the conflict *(via VanWyngarden)*

Following leave from mid-May, he returned in July, became *Staffelführer*, and suddenly hit his stride flying the D VII, which he recalled as 'the best German scout machine of the war'. In August Becker downed two fighters, in September five bombers and in October three fighters and one two-seater. His 23rd, and final, kill (an American SPAD XIII of the 22nd Aero) came on 3 November 1918. He was nominated for the 'Blue Max' but did not receive it due to the Kaiser's abdication.

Vzfw Otto Klaiber went through the usual mill of two-seater operations before being considered as a fighter pilot. However, he and his observer with FA 232 had downed a French SPAD on 22 December 1917, and so in 1918 his request for single-seaters was acknowledged. Klaiber did not get to *Jasta* 12 until September 1918, but with the D VII he shot down five aircraft before the war had ended – three DH 4 bombers, two SPAD fighters and one SPAD two-seater.

His final victory – an American SPAD on 30 October – may have been flown by the US Aero ace Lt James D Beane, serving with the 22nd Aero Squadron (Ulrich Neckel may also have downed the American). The previous day Beane had scored his fifth and sixth victories which brought him a posthumous DSC to add to his French *Croix de Guerre*.

Ltn Alfred Greven was nearly an ace, surviving the war with four victories. He had been awarded the Saxon Albert Order, Knight 2nd Class with Swords and then the Saxon Merit Order. Proposed for the Knight's Cross of the Military St Henry Order, the war ended before it could be ratified. Greven had been flying with Hermann Becker on 18 September and again on 26 September, each action resulting in five victories. The first attack had been on DH 4s of the US 11th Aero Squadron, in which Becker scored a double, and Greven one for his second victory. Another pilot in this action was Ltn Hans Besser, who claimed his first victory. These three were also involved in the 26th action against DH 4s of the 20th Aero Squadron, Becker again getting two and Greven and Besser one each. The latter pilot recorded;

'The earth was almost completely covered by balls of clouds and the holes in between were very hazy. We were high above it at 4000 metres, and searched the sky for enemies. The weather looked to us as if it had been made for bombing attacks, for it allowed a covered approach between the clouds. And really, we had not been mistaken. Cleverly they flew around every mountain of cloud and stayed in the valleys, thereby using the change of light and shadow as camouflage. The colourful cockades, however, had betrayed them to us, and we dived vertically down onto them. What then happened occurred within a matter of seconds.

26 September 1918 – a happy day for *Jasta* 12 and a disastrous one for the US 20th Aero Squadron. Seven DH 4s from the American unit were attacked by Fokkers of *Jasta* 12, and five were shot down behind German lines, while one of the remaining two returned with a dead observer. The bomber flown by Lts G B Wiser (pilot) and G Richardson was forced to land directly on *Jasta* 12's airfield at Giraumont by Alfred Greven, giving the ace the second of his four victories. Here, Wiser (in the foreground by the wicker chairs with his back to the camera) and Richardson (next to Wiser, facing the camera) are surrounded by *Jasta* 12 personnel, including JG II *Kommandeur* Oblt Von Boenigk (officer at right with his hand in his pocket) *(via VanWyngarden)*

'We fell onto the formation like a hailstorm and the observers hardly had time to fire at us. We used the Fokker's speed to hang immediately at their tails. Almost all of us had an enemy in front of us. Becker and myself fire almost simultaneously at two Americans, but mine waits to take fire while Becker is so fast he had already produced the first torch in the sky. Almost at the same moment Becker's second victim is also on fire, as is my American. And of the other enemies there's also nothing to be seen any more, only some thick pillars of smoke stand above the clouds. Below us there are the burning machines, almost in a row, and some kilometres to the front another two.'

In Besser's account of the 26 September action he recorded how he had watched as the observer in the DH 4 he had attacked climbed onto the fuselage edge and then jumped headlong into space. He had faced sure death anyway and chose a quicker, less painful end. Just as he fell, the burning bomber exploded.

Jasta 13

Synonymous with *Jasta* 13 was the name of Franz Büchner, from Leipzig. Born on 2 January 1898, the son of a wealthy businessman, he joined the Army in 1914, serving with a Saxon infantry regiment on the Ypres sector while still only 16 years of age. Later that same year he contracted typhoid fever but in 1915 was back, this time on the Russian front, until he returned to France in 1916, having been commissioned in the field.

Wounded on 3 April, Büchner, like so many others, transferred to aviation, and after pilot training served in a two-seater unit prior to becoming a fighter pilot with *Jasta* 9 in March 1917. He served with the

unit through to September. A month after he gained his first victory, on 17 August, he was posted to *Jasta* 13. He gained victory number two on 15 October, but he had to wait until 10 June 1918 for his third, by which time D VIIs were arriving and *Jasta* 13 was part of JG II.

On 15 June the leader of *Jasta* 13, Ltn Wilhelm Schwartz (eight victories) was wounded, and it fell to Büchner to take over. Some *Jastas* seemed to have one or two 'star turns' (aces) who were supported by the rest of the pilots, and *Jasta* 13 is a good example. Büchner was to end the war with a very creditable 40 victories, 36 of them as *Staffelführer*. *Jasta* 13 included four other aces in its ranks during this period. These were Ulrich Neckel (already an ace with *Jasta* 12), Alfred Haussman (he too was already an ace by the summer of 1917), Kurt Hetze and Werner Neithammer. Other pilots picked up the odd one or two kills, but of the 108 official victories claimed, Büchner's share was 37 per cent. His fifth victory came on 28 June 1918, and by the end of July he had downed 12.

D VIIs began to arrive in July in small numbers. On the 1st, for instance, *Jasta* 13 received two D VIIs. JG II received 20 more on the 14th, nine going to *Jasta* 12, three to *Jasta* 13 and eight to *Jasta* 19.

Although for the first time in many months JG II was now

Ltn Franz Büchner's 20th victory (on 20 August 1918) was the occasion for this group photo of *Jasta* 13. *Staffelführer* Büchner is seated on the left, directly beneath the nose of his D VII (OAW). Third from left is Ltn d R Grimm (three victories) and third from the right is Ltn d R Werner Niethammer (six victories) *(via VanWyngarden)*

Ulrich Neckel had served in *Jasta* 12 in September 1917, starting out as a lowly gefreiter. Promotions came along with his rapidly rising score, and by 10 July 1918 he was a leutnant with 19 victories. On that day he received confirmation for his 20th success, and posed for this dated photo. It was a popular custom in JG II for pilots to mark significant 'decade' victories with a floral wreath-decorated Fokker and the obligatory photo *(via VanWyngarden)*

Less than a month after his 20th victory, Franz Büchner reached his 30th on 18 September, and then posed for the usual 'photo op'. Here, his D VII (OAW) shows the louvred panel typical of the 4450-4649/18 batch. The plaque hanging from the greenery combined his green/white chequerboard with his 'werewolf's' head emblem, both of which were painted on the fuselage of his D VIIs. Büchner's wound badge – apparently in silver – is also visible *(via VanWyngarden)*

equipped with just one fighter type, difficulties remained. Petrol for the aircraft was becoming scarce and rationing was being imposed. Pilot numbers were also down, not helped by the first signs of the Spanish influenza epidemic which was about to inflict itself on the world.

20 August saw Büchner claim victory No 20 (in fact two victories), and during September he scored at a phenomenal rate – 17 successes took his score to 37. He received several Saxon awards, but his well-deserved *Pour le Mérite* was not announced until 25 October, by which time he had brought his score to 40. Büchner also survived a mid-air collision with one of his pilots on 10 October, both men successfully taking to their parachutes.

Büchner's glory days were during the fighting over the French and American offensives in September 1918. He often scored in multiples – three on 12 September, two on the 13th, 14th and 15th, a single on the 17th, followed by a triple on the 18th, four on the 26th and a single (his 17th kill of the month) on the 28th. Nine of these were SPAD XIIIs, mostly American flown, whilst the others were a smattering of Bréguet, Salmson and DH 4 bombers/recce aircraft. Of the four he shot down on 26 September, one each had come from the 22nd, 27th, 49th and 94th Aero Squadrons.

Ltn d R Werner Niethammer recorded his thoughts about his CO, Franz Büchner. He recalled the time the young 19-year-old tyro had scored his fifth victory, and had clearly begun to learn his trade;

'After his fifth victory he jumped out of his machine and came running over to us and shouted at once "Now I've found it out, men!" And he really had "found it out", for since that day they fell left and right. He scored doubles as well as his famous record of five (sic – four confirmed) in one day. He stood before us, tall and slender, with a youthful face. Yet there was a serious look in his eyes which raised a surmise that in this 19-year-old boy was hidden a leader's nature. He was a good comrade, happy, always in for fun, and helpful in any situation. Now what was the real reason for his success? In flying, Büchner wasn't that much superior to us as it looked from the difference in the number of victories. Turns and manoeuvres in the fight we knew also. So he was only that much better in deciding the moment – the moment when you smelled the enemy's castor oil and pushed the button. And that moment he'd found out.

'He was probably the best shot I've ever seen, and had a brilliant eye. How fast and well-aimed he fired! He demonstrated this to me on 29 July.

Jasta 13 Kommandeur Franz Büchner flew this flamboyantly decorated D VII (OAW) in the autumn of 1918. The serial number is not known, but the cowling panels would indicate a machine from the 6300-6649/18 sequence. The unit's dark green nose was bordered by a white band, and the fuselage was painted blue. Büchner's personal emblem of a chequerboard band in green and white (indicative of his native Saxony) and a leonine 'werewolf's' head are boldly displayed. Note the flare pistol tube and the additional sights mounted in front of the guns. The wings were covered in four-colour fabric (via VanWyngarden)

An evocative view of the deadly young Jasta 13 ace Franz Büchner, taking off in his D VII (OAW). The unit and personal markings are in full display (via VanWyngarden)

This early Fokker-built D VII of Werner Niethammer (whose name translates as 'riveting hammer') of Jasta 13 was decorated with his individual white hammer motif. It also bore the early style of simple green and dark blue Staffel markings. The crosses were altered from a previous form, resulting in the unusual style seen on the rudder. A rear-view mirror has been mounted on the wing centre section (via VanWyngarden)

We flew directly under the clouds, and because of the low height of the clouds – 700 metres – we flew in two flights of five machines each. Suddenly, an American came out of the clouds to my left, not even 300 metres off. I saw him at once. When I turned to attack him, Büchner had already hung on his propeller, after a steep left-hand turn, and managed

to fire a burst of seven rounds from each gun, before his Fokker nosed down. The American was a mass of flames, and the victory was officially confirmed as his 12th.'

Büchner flew during the immediate post-war revolution in Germany, serving with the Reichswehr. However, he was killed during a reconnaissance mission near his hometown of Leipzig on 18 March 1920, aged just 22. Like his JG II commander Berthold, he had survived the Great War only to die at the hands of fellow Germans. Indeed, he only survived Berthold by three days.

Ltn Werner Niethammer arrived just as Fokker biplanes were equipping the *Jasta*. Between 9 June and 22 October he accounted for six Allied aircraft – a Camel and five French and American two-seaters, with one SPAD unconfirmed. The latter victory was *Jasta* 13's final war kill, taking its tally to 124. Little is known of this ace other than he died in 1946. He did, however, leave a graphic account of the action on 10 August 1918;

'We were lying in front of our tents on our cots, awaiting take-off orders. As usual Büchner was lazily blinking into the sun. If he saw just one black dot of flak in the sky he would cry "Let's go men, get ready!", and then things could get rather unpleasant if we didn't get to our

Werner Niethammer's later D VII (OAW) bore his white hammer on both the sides and top of the fuselage. It also displays the later form of *Jasta* 13 unit marking – the area of the green colour on the nose was reduced and bordered in white, a change instituted by Büchner. Note the light rib tapes on the four-colour fabric wing and Niethammer's reinforced parachute harness (*via VanWyngarden*)

Jagdstaffel 13 pilots confer before a flight. Third from left is the youthful, but accomplished, commander Franz Büchner, and fourth from left is his brother Felix. On the extreme right, with goggles and scarf, is Werner Niethammer. Each of the pilots in flight gear are wearing the Heinecke harness, with Niethammer's showing the leather reinforcements and broad leg straps issued after some early harnesses failed (*via VanWyngarden*)

Ltn d R Werner Niethammer attained six victories with *Jasta* 13, at least five of which were probably scored in D VIIs. His writings provide colourful accounts of his comrades in the *Staffel* (via VanWyngarden)

The first form of *Jasta* 13 unit marking is demonstrated on the Fokker flown by the 15-victory ace Vzfw Albert Haussmann. The nose was painted a dark green back to a point roughly in line with the ammunition chutes for the guns. The rest of the fuselage and horizontal tail surfaces were the usual JG II dark blue. Haussmann's personal embellishment was the engrailed fuselage band in two colours, possibly red and black (via VanWyngarden)

aeroplanes at top speed, to sit in the cockpits awaiting the take-off signal.

'Right after take-off we ran into bad weather – low cloud and poor visibility. In the Laon sector we got into a dogfight in which Büchner shot down a two-seater (his 14th victory – author) and got himself put out of commission – that is, he received some hits in his fuel tank. The fuel leaked out and soaked him from top to bottom. He did have the presence of mind to switch off the engine. Still, it was quite a bit of luck that he didn't get burned up. He landed somewhere in the terrain in the middle of the retreat operations and latched on to the last two machine gunners dropping back.'

Jasta 13 became scattered and after inadvertently chasing a Frenchman, thinking him a comrade, Niethammer found himself over enemy positions;

'Soon I spotted an army camp, which I decided to examine to see if I could possibly land there. I corkscrewed down, only to find that I was tangling with tanks. I levelled off and strafed the camp, sending horses and wagons scattering in all directions. Soon they were giving me such a plastering with their machine guns that I had to beat a hasty retreat. I received 30 hits in my aeroplane and landed at the base of the Richthofen *Geschwader*. I needed new wheels, since the tyres had been shot up.

'Just as we sat down to discuss the next move, an orderly ran up and reported to all *Staffel* leaders present that enemy artillery was approaching the aerodrome. We ran outside, and sure enough there they were at the very edge of the field already. No airfield was left in such as hurry as we left that one.'

Towards the end of the war, Franz Büchner's brother Felix joined the *Jasta*. On 13 September he downed a SPAD, with another unconfirmed, followed by a Caudron R 11 on the 14th. On 10 October Felix and Gftr Michaelis collided in combat, but both survived by parachute descent from around 12,000 ft.

Vzfw Albert Haussmann came from Stuttgart, born on 10 October 1892. In 1916 he had flown with KG 3, gaining one combat victory – a French Caudron – which he shared with his observer. He then moved to *Schusta* 8 and finally became a fighter pilot with *Jasta* 23 in April 1917. Following three victories here, Haussmann moved to *Jasta* 15 in June, where he became an ace with his fifth and sixth kills on 13 August.

His final move was to *Jasta* 13 in the summer of 1918, just as the unit was starting to fly Fokker biplanes. At some point in July Haussmann narrowly survived a mid-air collision in which the rudder and one elevator of his D VII were destroyed – he kept his nerve and managed to land the crippled aircraft, emerging with minor head injuries. By 26 September he had scored a total of 15 victories, at least seven of which had been scored in a D VII. However, on 16 October (six days after his 26th birthday) this experienced NCO pilot was killed while strafing Allied trenches. His wingman Werner Niethammer wrote;

'When Haussmann flew up to me after an attack at about 700 metres, I suddenly saw his machine smoking. Right after that he baled out. His parachute must have gotten damaged during the jump because it didn't open properly, but formed itself into a sort of pear shape. Haussmann broke his neck upon striking the ground. It is possible that he had been hit from the ground. But it could just as easily have been one of those cases of spontaneous combustion of the ammunition or the fuel which also cost our Uffz Laabs his life.'

Ltn Kurt Hetze became an ace flying the Fokker biplanes of *Jasta* 13, although his early kills may have been scored before the unit was fully equipped. However, at least three of his five victories, plus one

In July 1918, Albert Haussmann of *Jasta* 13 survived a mid-air collision in his D VII. The rudder and elevators of his Fokker were severely damaged, yet he still managed to crash land the crippled machine, emerging with only a minor head injury. Haussman is seen on the extreme left, his head heavily bandaged
(via VanWyngarden)

A formal portrait of well-decorated *Jasta* 13 ace Ltn d R Kurt Hetze. He is seen wearing the Saxon award of the Knight's Cross 2nd Class with Swords badge of the Merit and Albert Order, the Iron Cross 1st and 2nd Class and the Silver Wound Badge, indicating three or four wounds *(via VanWyngarden)*

The men of *Jasta* 18 pose for the camera prior to joining *Jasta* 15 en masse. This unit change was brought about by *Jasta* 18's former commander, Rudolf Berthold, seen here sitting in the centre of the front row. The other pilots in this shot are, standing, from left to right, Schafer (11 kills), Runge (8 kills), Turck (10 kills), Dingel and Rahn (6 kills), and seated, left to right, Strähle (15 kills), Veltjens (35 kills), Auffahrt (30 kills) and Schober *(via VanWyngarden)*

unconfirmed, were certainly scored in the D VII, as he had arrived at the *Jasta* in June 1918. The unconfirmed claim – a two-seater from the 12th US Aero Squadron – was probably the aircraft flown by Maj Louis Brereton, which crash landed inside American lines on 12 September. Brereton survived to become a USAAF general in World War 2, commanding the Ninth Air Force in the Mediterranean.

The day after this action, Hetze found himself in a car with some comrades on a trip to the battle front. What happened during this excursion Hetze recorded himself;

'Because we had not yet had confirmation of the six Americans of the previous day, we wanted to try and obtain them at the front from the infantry. Therefore, I ordered a car from the *Staffel*, and when I left the mess I jokingly said "Now I will drive to the front and will get my wound badge".

'The two Büchners, Niethammer and von Hantelmann (*Jasta* 15 – author) all piled in with me and away we went to the front. We had no idea of the fact that our retreat from the St Mihiel salient was being made right then. Suddenly, we were fired at near Woël by a low flying SPAD. Out we went and somebody shouted "Not under the car!" Before we knew it, the fellow was a few metres over our heads. We flung ourselves into the shallow ditch next to the road and peered upwards. Stones from the machine gun burst flew around. In the second pass I was wounded – hit in the lungs! Hardly had I risen when the fellow came back and fired at us again.'

Hetze did not return to operational flying. Ironically, the unidentified SPAD pilot had just missed ending the careers of four other formidable JG II pilots.

Jasta 15

Staffel 15 had a brief moment of unusual history in the early days of the *Geschwader*. Following Rudolf Berthold's appointment, he had tried to get his old *Jasta* 18 to become part of JG II, but this would have meant one of the other *Jasta* units being moved out – something which, on this occasion, did not get *Kofl's* approval. Yet somehow he managed to have all the flying personnel exchanged. That is to say all of the existing *Jasta* 15 men were sent to *Jasta* 18, whilst all the *Jasta* 18 pilots were posted in to *Jasta* 15! From this distance in time it seems inexplicable, for if this massed transfer was indeed condoned, wouldn't it have been easier just to swap *Jasta* 15 for *Jasta* 18 en-masse?

Jasta 15's CO at the time of the swap had been Ltn August Raben, although another *Jasta* 15 man, Oblt Ernst Wilhelm Turck, then assumed command until 18 May

Accompanied by his faithful Alsatian dog 'Bella', Ltn Josef 'Seppl' Veltjens poses for the traditional portrait with his decorated D VII to commemorate his 20th victory, which he had achieved as part of a double on 11 June. Veltjens, a loyal protégé of Berthold, was commander of *Jasta* 15 at this time. Veltjens' D VII was a Fokker-built example, and it still bore fully-bordered crosses on the wings at this stage. The struts seem to be light grey. When JG II was stationed at Balatré in April, 'Bella' gave birth to puppies, one of which was adopted by von Hantelmann and christened 'Seppl'!
(via VanWyngarden)

This time, Josef Veltjens' Fokker was not bedecked to celebrate a significant 'decade' victory, but rather the *Staffel* commander's 24th birthday on 2 June 1918. Veltjens' well-known personal emblem of a white 'Indian arrow' is seen on the fuselage, and the light struts may be noted. The blue/red demarcation on the fuselage is well evident. An anemometer-type airspeed indicator was mounted on the port interplane 'N' strut *(HAC/UTD via VanWyngarden)*

1918, at which time one of Berthold's men, Josef 'Seppl' Veltjens, took command.

Ltn Veltjens was born on 2 June 1894 in Geldern, west of Duisberg. A soldier in a guards regiment at the start of the war, then a grenadier, he became an NCO prior to a request to join the Air Service. In May 1916 Veltjens went to the front as a two-seater pilot and quickly received a commission for his good reconnaissance work. In March 1917 he was posted to *Jasta* 14, where he became a protégé of Berthold's.

His first five victories had been scored by 1 June, and then he followed Berthold to *Jasta* 18, where he brought his score to ten early in 1918. Then came the wholesale move, and by 25 June 1918 Veltjens had achieved 23 victories, having become *Staffelführer* on 18 May. Now in line for the *Pour le Mérite*, he had to wait until 16 August for this to be approved and awarded, by which time his score had risen to 30 – his 29th and 30th kills came that same day.

Twice Veltjens held temporary command of JG II during von Boenigk's leave periods, so paperwork often interrupted his flying.

Fokkers of JG II are seen scattered around the aerodrome at Chéry-les-Pouilly in August 1918. *Jasta* 15 leader Veltjens' D VII is parked in the foreground, marked with a white arrow and two stripes on the blue tailplane to distinguish the commander's aircraft. In the middle distance is a line of white-nosed Fokkers of *Jasta* 12, with Greven's lightning-bolt marked D VII (OAW). Behind them can be seen *Jasta* 13 machines
(*HAC/UTD via VanWyngarden*)

However, during October he brought his score to 35, flying not only the Fokker biplane but occasionally the Siemens-Schuckert D III. Veltjens served in the Luftwaffe during World War 2, attaining the rank of colonel, and at one period served as Hermann Göring's emissary to Finland. He was killed on 6 October 1943 in a flying accident whilst a passenger in a Ju 52/3m transport.

Whilst Veltjens was acting leader of JG II, *Jasta* 15 was led by Ltn Oliver Freiherr von Beaulieu-Marconnay, whom we shall also read about under *Jasta* 19. Born in Berlin-Charlottenburg on 14 September 1898, he was the son of a Prussian army captain. A student, aged 16, at the time of hostilities, he enrolled as a cadet with a dragoon regiment and saw action on the Eastern Front. Commissioned at 17, von Beaulieu-Marconnay continued with the dragoons until transferring to aviation in 1917, and on 1 December received a posting to *Jasta* 15.

'Beauli' scored his first victory on 28 May 1918 and seven more in June. By the time he was flying D VIIs the Battle of Amiens had begun, and this presented the 19-year-old with more targets in the air, so by the end of August his tally was into double figures. He formed a close friendship with Georg von Hantelmann and Hugo Schaefer – the

The youthful and loquacious Ltn Oliver Freiherr von Beaulieu-Marconnay strikes a happy pose with his BMW-engined Fokker. While often captioned as a *Jasta* 19 photo, this view is now believed to show von Beaulieu during his earlier service in *Jasta* 15. The white *4D* was the branding iron emblem of the pilot's former *Dragoner-Regiment 'von Bredow' (1. Schlesisches) Nr 4*, or the 4th Dragoon Regiment (the same unit as Lothar von Richthofen). It is suggested that this aircraft may previously have been one of Berthold's machines, as his emblem seems to be visible beneath the overpaint. The uppersurface of the top wing may be dark blue as well, although the 'white' area on the starboard wing is unexplained. Note the high-mounted machine guns and the windscreen, and the cowling panel bears evidence of considerable louvre modification
(*via VanWyngarden*)

'Three Inseparables' as they were called. The talkative young ex-dragoon decorated his aircraft with the '4D' branding iron emblem of his former 4th Dragoon regiment. On 2 September, however, von Beaulieu-Marconnay had to leave his close companions at *Jasta* 15 to take command of *Jasta* 19.

Ltn Georg von Hantelmann was another exceptional fighter pilot in *Jasta* 15. And if Franz Büchner of *Jasta* 13 had been deemed young, then von Hantelmann was, by nine months, even younger, born on 9 October 1898. He joined the military in 1916, and on 15 June was

commissioned into the *Braun-schweiger* Hussar Regiment Nr 17 – the 'Death's Head Hussars' (the Death's Head insignia would decorate his Fokker). However, he soon transferred into the air service, and following his training he was sent to *Jasta* 18 on 6 February 1918, aged 19. By the time of the personnel swap von Hantelmann had yet to record his first victory, but he finally did so on 6 June – a British DH 4 bomber. By the end of that month he had four victories, plus three more unconfirmed, but when he received the D VII he really started to score.

Von Beaulieu-Marconnay in a serious mood, in front of his D VII. On 2 September he left *Jasta* 15 to take command of *Jasta* 19. On 18 October, whilst attacking a SPAD, he was accidentally wounded by fire from a *Jasta* 74 D VII. He died eight days later, the announcement of his 'Blue Max' arriving six hours after his death *(via VanWyngarden)*

Two kills came in August, then 12 during September, including three on the 14th against the Americans. Seven more kills followed in October, and his 25th, and final, claim on 4 November almost got him the 'Blue Max', but the Kaiser's abdication made him miss out. Surviving the war at just a month past his 20th birthday, von Hantelmann was fated to die at the hands of Polish poachers on his estates in East Prussia on 7 September 1924.

Von Hantelmann's prowess in aerial combat is shown by some of the important Allied airmen he brought down. On 12 September 1918 he shot down Lt David Putnam, a 13-victory ace (with many probables) flying with the US 139th Aero Squadron – Putnam was two months younger than his German adversary, but he had already more than proved himself in action with both the French and the American air forces. On the 16th *Jasta* 15 attacked two SPADs that had just flamed a balloon, and Hantelmann brought down the one flown by the French ace Sous-Lt Maurice Boyau of SPA77, who had just moments before attained his 35th

On 17 June 1918, Ltn Georg von Hantelmann's *Jasta* 15 D VII was borrowed by new arrival Kurt Wüsthoff for a fateful patrol. The flight of JG II aircraft engaged 15 SE 5as from No 24 Sqn, and Wüsthoff was brought down with a serious groin wound, landing the D VII behind French lines to become a prisoner. The fighter was turned over to the British, who gave it the number G/5/17 Bde. The D VII duly became the subject of great study. When in German hands, its military serial number had been 382/18, and the Fokker *Werke* number 2469. The fighter was fitted with a high-compression Mercedes engine, Nr 41245. The emblem on the fuselage signified von Hantelmann's service in the *Braunschweiger* Hussar Regiment Nr 17, one of the famous 'Death's Head Hussar' regiments. The fuselage cross is still slightly visible through the coat of dark blue paint, and the wings retained their factory five-colour fabric finish *(via VanWyngarden)*

Another photo of von Hantelmann's D VII 382/18 being salvaged by RAF personnel. Note the low-level exhaust manifold, typical of early Fokker products *(via VanWyngarden)*

For some reason, photos of Ltn d R Georg von Hantelmann are scarce. One of the best shows the youthful ace posing for the cameraman in typical JG II fashion to mark his 20th victory, this photograph being taken on 9 October 1918 at Charmois aerodrome. On 4 November 1918, von Hantelmann claimed his final victory in D VII 465/18, but it is not known if this is indeed that aircraft *(HAC/UTD via VanWyngarden)*

victory. On the 18th he downed Joseph Wehner, the six-kill wingman and friend of Frank Luke Jr, who flew with the 27th Aero Squadron.

One of his comrades in *Jasta* 15, Ltn Joachim von Zeigesar (three victories), wrote about his friend Georg in 1933 for Hantelmann's sister Anna-Louise Bardt's memoirs of her brother (translated for us by O'Brien Browne). He described von Hantelmann's first victory, scored on 6 June – he mistakenly described their opponents as Frenchmen, for it seems they were certainly British DH 4s;

'We are standing around the airfield and talking when suddenly the report arrives from our radio position that an enemy formation of seven aircraft is nearing our area. With inimitable speed, we are dressed and sitting in our machines. Before every flight, the engine is first "braked" – a hellish noise – then the machines are rolling for take off. Veltjens, as leader, raises his hand and the wild chase is on. After a few minutes the *Staffel* is in its usual order. While we climb with full running engines, "Seppl" leads us to the front so that we cut off the enemy's way back. Soon we are at 4000 metres, then we catch sight of them. Our aircraft are fast and our wills are like iron to get the "cockades".

'Veltjens gives us the signal to attack! Like a steer unbound, the aircraft with the Braunschweig

Hussar's crest dives into the enemy first. Even before we others have a chance to shoot, Hantelmann goes down with his left wingman on the Frenchmen (sic) flying in arrow formations. For us, there isn't any more time left to watch. Each one grabs hold of his opponent and, as it is normal in air fighting, only a few minutes pass by and the French squadron that was in the process of returning home no longer exists! Radiating joy, we gather together again around our leader and try, flushed with victory, to find new battles.

'Having landed, we have hardly climbed out of our machines when the usual victory claim dispute arises. Everyone has to tell his story. It is determined, though, that Hantelmann was the first one to bag his opponent. And the joy is all the greater because exactly in this flight not only he but also I achieved my first incontestable aerial victory.

'We all painted our aircraft in the same way. Everything, even the wings (sic), was dark blue – only the engine cowlings were red, up to the pilot's seat. This was supposed to be an allusion to the old German infantry uniform, because Hptm Berthold had belonged to the Prussian Infantry Regiment Nr 20. In order for us to be able to identify one another in the air, each aircraft carried an identification mark on the side of the fuselage in white paint. Thus for Hantelmann a blue and yellow coat of arms with his regiment's death's head, Veltjens' feathered arrow, Schäfer's horrible yet beautiful snake, and so on.'

In July *Jasta* 15 and JG II were in the Champagne offensive. Von Ziegesar wrote;

'In quick time Hantelmann shot down one opponent after the other, and it was characteristic that these were mostly enemy fighter aircraft, which he took care of in his impetuous, daredevil style. On 9 October 1918, the memorable flight happened in which he achieved his 20th victory, and was recommended for the *Pour le Mérite*. It was so nice in our circle of comrades that the joy about this victory was shared without jealousy from the others.

'Then the sad time for us followed in which petrol became so short that we could only fly under great restrictions. For these reasons we mostly

After the war's end, Ltn d R Hugo Schäfer's Fokker wound up in American hands. It bore standard *Jasta* 15 red and dark blue coloration, and Schäfer's personal blazon of a white winged snake. Again, the dark blue *Staffel* paint still permits the fuselage cross to show through slightly. Other photos of this machine reveal that the snake emblem was repeated on the upper deck of the fuselage, albeit in a somewhat simpler design. Close comrades Schäfer, von Hantelmann and Beaulieu-Marconnay formed a trio known as the 'three inseparables' *(via VanWyngarden)*

flew in twos, so that at least our aeroplanes were always at the front in order to protect our own working aircraft. The French and Americans, who used to be located across from us, often flew in formations of 50 or more aircraft, but it was nevertheless difficult for us to get a shot.

'One day, however, we were successful in engaging a strong French flight in aerial combat, which soon broke up into individual fights. When we gathered together again Hantelmann was missing. Finally, we discovered him well below us, as he roared behind a Frenchman at a wild speed. Only very seldom did we see the smoke trails of the phosphorus ammunition that indicated he was firing. The chase went lower and lower, until finally the Frenchman smashed to pieces in the swamps on the banks of the Maas, and only the tail of the fuselage protruded out of the mire.

'During another flight we were both alone. We had discovered a squadron of two-seaters which was flying above us towards German territory. As we were gaining height, we pushed in between them and the front in order to be able to still get at them on their return flight. All at once, Hantelmann disappeared downwards from my side in a rushing dive, and while I was still above covering where an enemy single-seater flight was coming up at us, he got two enemy single-seaters in one minute – which perhaps had felt themselves safe so far over their lines – even before I had a chance to follow him. Burning, both crashed down right next to each other into the deep, and we rushed over to our side of the front because we had come down very low, and a huge number of enemy combat aircraft were coming down after us.

'We saw one another only rarely after the war because he was in Munich and I further north. All the more, it was a very special pleasure for me when he asked me to attend his marriage in Potsdam, which will always remain a festive memory for me.

'One thing is certain. No better memorial to our Georg von Hantelmann can be set up than has been erected in the steadfast, loyal thoughts of him as a hero and as a beloved person, by the respect in the hearts of his old comrades.'

Hantelmann's first 'Death's Head'-marked D VII became famous for another reason on 17 June 1918. D VII 382/18 was flown that day by Ltn Kurt Wüsthoff, a 27-victory ace formerly with *Jasta* 4. Until recently he had been on the staff of JG II, but on 16 June this *Pour le Mérite* winner was given command of *Jasta* 15. The very next day, having borrowed the D VII, he was shot down and wounded in combat with several pilots of No 24 Sqn. He and the Fokker survived, but were down in Allied lines,

A splendid line-up of *Jasta* 15 Fokkers reveal a variety of personal markings. From the left are seen Vzfw Klaudat's D VII marked with his Uhlan lance with a black and white pennon, then Joachim von Ziegesar's machine with his three white feathers, then von Beaulieu-Marconnay's aircraft with his *4D* symbol. The final aircraft bears an unidentified crowned crest *(via VanWyngarden)*

where he became a prisoner – the D VII became a prized trophy, given the RAF code G/5/17 Bde.

Ltn Hugo Schäfer was another *Jasta* 18/15 transferee, born in Eberfeld on 30 June 1894. He joined the military in early 1915 and was commissioned in July. After pilot training Schäfer arrived at *Jasta* 18 in March 1918, scoring two quick victories before the month was out, and a third on 1 April – the day the Royal Air Force was formed.

His next eight victories were all claimed in his D VII, although he was shot down on 17 June during the fight in which his new commander Wüsthoff was brought down, but Schäfer landed on the right side of the trenches. He flew a D VII emblazoned with a white winged snake. His final victory came on 9 October – his fourth SPAD kill – which he added to his one SE 5 and six Allied two-seaters. Surviving the war, Schäfer was killed in a flying accident on 3 February 1920.

Vzfw Gustav Klaudat was in the fight along with von Hantelmann which resulted in Maurice Boyau's fall on 16 September. He shot down Boyau's wingman, Cpl Walk. Although he claimed an unconfirmed kill on 1 October, the victory over Walk proved to be Klaudat's sixth and final confirmed success.

A modest but popular East Prussian, Klaudat had served in a Uhlan regiment prior to moving to flying, and arrived at *Jasta* 15 during July 1918. Like von Hantelmann and Von Beaulieu-Marconnay, he used a fuselage marking emblematic of his former cavalry service – a black/white Uhlan lance and pennant. Klaudat was wounded in the left arm on 23 October whilst attacking Bréguet bombers of the 96th Aero Squadron (although he has also been credited to Rickenbacker of the 94th Aero Squadron), and this put him out of the war.

Ltn Johannes Klein became a fighter pilot in February 1917, joining *Jasta* 27, then moving to *Jasta* 18 in August. His first two victories were scored with *Jasta* 27 in the summer of 1917, and he then became involved in the pilot swap with *Jasta* 15. By the time D VIIs began arriving Klein had around seven kills, and during the summer of 1918, he raised this to 16. His Fokker was reportedly marked with a white fuselage band. Klein was slightly wounded in combat on 15 September, which slowed him down a bit, but he survived the war. However, his death was reported in 1926.

Ltn Johannes Klein of *Jasta* 15 proudly wears his Knight's Cross with Swords of the Hohenzollern House Order – awarded on 19 September 1918 – in his tunic buttonhole. By that date he had achieved most of his 15 victories *(via VanWyngarden)*

Jasta 19

Ltn Hans Pippart took command of *Jasta* 19 following the loss of Walter Göttsch. Born in Mannheim on 14 May 1888, he had learnt to fly pre-war, and in fact had his own aircraft manufacturing company. Naturally, he joined the German Air Service, although he was retained as an instructor until early 1916, at which time he became a two-seater pilot on the Russian Front. Pippart was commissioned in November and then in April 1917 he was assigned to fly single-seaters with *Kampfstaffel* I of *Sudarmee Jagdkommando*.

His first six victories – four balloons and two aircraft – were scored on the Russian Front, and in December he moved to the Western Front to fly with *Jasta* 13. On 20 April 1918 he took command of *Jasta* 19, and by

Jasta 19 *Staffelführer* **Ltn d L Hans Pippart celebrates his 21st (and penultimate) victory of 22 July in the time-honoured JG II fashion. The D VII (OAW) probably bore** *Jasta* 19 **colours of a chrome yellow nose and dark blue fuselage, but sadly no personal markings can be seen. A flare pistol and cartridge rack are attached to the cockpit side. Pippart flamed a balloon on 11 August for his 22nd victory, but died later that day, another victim of a failed parachute jump** *(HAC/UTD via VanWyngarden)*

the time Fokker biplanes began to arrive in the early summer, his score had reached 15. On 11 August he downed a balloon to bring his total kills to 22 (a figure which included seven balloons), but during an aerial fight over Noyon, his D VII was crippled. Taking to his parachute, he fell to his death when it failed to open.

Ulrich Neckel then took command of *Jasta* 19, adding three D VII victories to his *Jasta* 12 and 13 tally of 21, before leaving to take over the leadership of *Jasta* 6 on 1 September.

Neckel's place was taken by Ltn Oliver Freiherr von Beaulieu-Marconnay of *Jasta* 15, whose exploits we read about earlier. By this time 'Beauli' was an experienced fighter ace, and he continued to score with his new command. In September 1918 he increased his personal tally from 13 to 21, and in October raised this to 25. He was another of the *Geschwader's* 'youngsters', and like Büchner and von Hantelmann, was only 19 whilst with *Jasta* 15. Von Beaulieu-Marconnay celebrated his 20th birthday on 14 September by shooting down a Bréguet XIV for his 17th kill.

However, on 16 October he was seriously wounded in an air battle – ironically, he was hit by fire from another German aircraft – although he survived his forced landing. His injuries gave grave concern that he would not survive, and so his *Pour le Mérite* was rushed through and he was informed of the award while in hospital shortly before his death on the 26th.

Jasta 19 had three other pilots who became aces with the arrival of the D VII, namely Ltns Hans Körner, Wilhelm Leusch and Rudolf Rienau. All three had seen considerable action prior to them joining *Jasta* 19.

Körner had joined *Jasta* 8 in January 1917 as an unteroffizier. He achieved one victory on 10 January (a British balloon on the Ypres front), then moved to *Jasta* 27 for a couple of weeks, but was then sent out to Macedonia to fly with a two-seater unit. On 30 June he scored his second kill. Returning to *Jasta* 8 in October as a vizefeldwebel, Körner shot down a Sopwith Pup for victory number three, then went to *Jasta* 19 and was commissioned.

Flying a Dr I triplane, he downed a SPAD next but then gained his fifth, sixth and seventh victories with a D VII in the final weeks of the war. With the coming of peace he remained in aviation, but was killed in a motorcycle crash while on his way to his airfield.

Wilhelm Leusch came from Neuss, south of Dusseldorf, born on 15 October 1892. He joined the flying services in October 1914 and was on two-seaters during 1915-16, at which time he was commissioned. Assigned to *Jasta* 13 in November, Leusch transferred to *Jasta* 19 in April 1917 and gained his first victory in May.

His second victory came in June 1918, and his last three were scored in the final weeks of the war whilst flying a D VII. On 18 October Leusch was given command of the *Staffel*, a position he held until the Armistice. He was killed in a glider crash on 14 August 1921.

Rudolf Rienau was born on the island of Sylt, off the German/Danish coast, on 17 November 1898. He was in the infantry from mid-1915, but by April 1917 had volunteered for pilot training. His first *staffel* was *Jasta* 1, which he joined in October of that same year, but he soon moved to *Jasta* 19, gaining his first victory in March 1918 and his second in June. Rienau's last four kills were achieved in D VIIs, giving him ace status.

He was lucky to survive being shot down on 13 September (a Friday) 1918, his D VII being hit by fire from an American SPAD north of Charey, but he successfully baled out – from just 500 metres – so his luck had not totally deserted him! His victor was a pilot from the 13th Aero Squadron, but as the Americans did not see him jump, he was only claimed as a probable. Rienau recorded;

'I took off for the lines with a flight of four Fokkers and attacked six SPADs at 3000 metres. While I was pursuing one, another grabbed me from behind and shot the cables and apparently the rudder in half. The aeroplane plunged downwards and just could not be brought out of it. At about 500 metres I tried one more time, but the seat broke and the Fokker nosed over into a left hand bank. Thereupon I unbuckled the safety belt, let myself flop out backwards to the left, banged my shoulder on the rudder, and after a very short fall, floated down. My aircraft lay about 150 metres from me, completely destroyed.'

Rienau remained flying after the war, but was killed while an instructor in a flying accident at Staaken, near Berlin, on 23 May 1925.

The final commander of *Jagdstaffel* 19 was Ltn d R Wilhelm Leusch, who was a veteran of the unit, having served continually from April 1917. He was credited with five victories, the last three scored in October-November 1918 *(via VanWyngarden)*

A stellar collection of eagles was caught by the camera in Berlin as they gathered for the final fighter trials at Adlershof in late October 1918. The Eversbusch brothers who owned the Pfalz firm courted the favour of these airmen just as eagerly as Anthony Fokker and others, and Alfred Eversbusch took this opportunity to be photographed with the nine aces seen here, most of whom were accomplished D VII exponents. The three current *Geschwader* commanders are seated in the front row, from left to right, Hermann Göring (JG I), his friend Bruno Loerzer (JG III) and Oskar Freiherr von Boenigk (JG II) – von Boenigk would soon receive his *Pour le Mérite* at these trials, but this had not yet occurred when this photo was taken. In the back row, from the left, are Hans Klein (formerly of *Jasta* 10, but out of action since being wounded in the right hand on 19 February – note the missing index finger), Josef Veltjens of *Jasta* 15, Eversbusch, Udet of *Jasta* 4 and Josef Jacobs of *Jasta* 7. All of these pilots would survive the war, and would be credited with over 250 Allied aircraft downed between them *(via VanWyngarden)*

LOERZER'S JG III – AND THE BAVARIANS

Royal Prussian JG III was formed on the same day as JG II – 2 February 1918. Its first, and only, *Kommandeur* was Hptm Bruno Loerzer, who took over on the 21st. His four *Jagdstaffeln* were 2 (Boelcke), 26, 27 and 36.

Bruno Loerzer, like his friend Hermann Göring, had been on active duty since the war began. Born on 22 January 1891, in Berlin, he was two years older than his friend, and Loerzer had been a cadet with an infantry regiment before attending Military School, being commissioned in January 1913, aged 22.

He began flying lessons prior to the war, and by October 1914 was a fully fledged pilot, and sent to *Feldfliegerabteilung* 25. On the 28th of that month he was joined by Göring, whom he had met pre-war in the same infantry regiment, and who now became his observer. They flew together until June 1915, at which time Göring went off to become a pilot himself, and following assignments with two other two-seater units, Loerzer

The only *Geschwader Kommandeur* of *Jagdgeschwader* III was Hptm Bruno Loerzer, who would survive the war with 44 victories. Under his leadership the BMW-powered D VIIs of JG III inflicted heavy losses on the RAF into late 1918
(via VanWyngarden)

Bruno Loerzer's famous D VII bore the black and white markings of his old *Jagdstaffel* 26 on its fuselage overall, and on the wings as well. Von Richthofen himself specified that a *Geschwader* leader's aircraft should be conspicuously marked to facilitate the leadership of large formations, and Loerzer obviously agreed. Black and white stripes were marked on the top of the upper wing and beneath the lower wing as well – the rest of the wings were covered in five-colour fabric. In addition, black/white streamers were affixed to the interplane struts. It may be noted that at least three *Geschwader* commanders – Göring, Berthold and Loerzer – flew highly decorated D VIIs, with colours extended to the wing surfaces
(via VanWyngarden)

A gleeful Friedrich Seekatz of the Fokker Company (far left) takes advantage of an opportunity to be photographed with some of the brightest stars of the *Jagdstaffeln*, who had gathered for another set of fighter trials in Berlin, circa late June 1918. These men are, from left to right, Seekatz, JG III commander Bruno Loerzer, Hermann Göring (soon to be JG I commander), Lothar von Richthofen (shortly before returning to the front for the final time), Ltn Hans Kirschstein of *Jasta* 6, with his newly-won 'Blue Max', Ltn d R Constantin Krefft (JG I technical officer), Ltn Friedrich Mallinckrodt (formerly of *Jasta* 6 and 20, now an advisor to *Idflieg*) and Fw Ltn Fritz Schubert (*Jasta* 6, also on the technical staff of JG I). Kirschstein would die in the crash of a Hannover two-seater on 16 July, only days after this photograph was taken *(via VanWyngarden)*

began to fly Eindeckers with Kek Jametz. He scored his first fighter victory on 21 March 1916 and ten days later his second.

Loerzer joined *Jasta* 5 upon its formation in the summer of 1916, then briefly moved to *Jasta* 17, but then, due to his rank and experience, was given command of *Jasta* 26 on 18 January 1917. He led this *staffel* until taking command of JG III, by which time he had achieved 23 victories. Two days after taking over JG III came the award of the *Pour le Mérite*. Leading JG III, Loerzer downed a further three Allied machines before the first Fokker D VIIs began to arrive. In July his score slowly mounted and victory No 30 came on 13 August. By the end of the month he had 34 confirmed claims.

During August 1918 JG III began to receive the superior BMW-engined D VIIs with which its pilots began to inflict severe damage on the RAF. During September alone, the unit claimed 130 victories, Loerzer raising his score to 44 by the 26th. Promoted to hauptmann on 10 October, he, like Göring over with JG I, seemed not to be too involved in combat in the final weeks of the war, and his September score of 44 was not improved upon.

After the war, with the emergence of the Luftwaffe in the 1930s, Göring made sure his friend joined the new force – he was already President of the German Air Sport Association. By the end of 1939 Loerzer had become a leutnant-general, adding the Knight's Cross of the Iron Cross to his decorations in May 1940. At one stage he held the position of Inspector of Fighters, and later he was made commander of Nr II *Fliegerkorps*, but to some rarely seemed effective. He rose to the rank of generaloberst and died on 23 August 1960.

Always intent on ingratiating himself with Germany's top fighter pilots, Anthony Fokker seems very happy to pose with JG III *Kommandeur* Bruno Loerzer (left) and eventual JG I leader Hermann Göring – both of whom display their *Pour le Mérite* decorations. The occasion was undoubtedly one of the various fighter competitions held in the summer/autumn of 1918 *(via VanWyngarden)*

JASTA BOELCKE

Loerzer had some formidable flyers in his *Geschwader*. *Jasta* 2 – known as *Jasta* Boelcke in memory of its first commander – had been at the forefront of the air fighting since its

Jasta Boelcke pilots in 1918. They are, from left to right, with known victories, Frey, Alfred Lindenberger (12), Otto Löffler (15), Wilhelm Suer (1), Mynereck (rear), Gerhard Bassenge (front, 5), Eberhard von Gudenberg, OzbV, Ernst Bormann (16), Karl Bolle (31), Hermann Frommherz (32) and Johann Heemsoth (2). By the end of the war, *Jasta* Boelcke was the second highest scoring *Jagdstaffel* of all, with 336 victories, the last of these being scored by Bolle on 4 November 1918 *(via VanWyngarden)*

Oblt Karl Bolle was the leader largely responsible for bringing the legendary *Jasta* Boelcke back to its status as a crack fighter *Staffel*. His Fokker D VII bore the unit markings of a black/white tailplane and white nose, along with his personal emblem on the fuselage – a broad yellow band reminiscent of his service in the *Kürassier-Regiment* 'von Seydlitz' Nr 7, flanked by bands in the black/white colours of Prussia. Most of the rest of the fuselage appears to be black. The two white bands on the upper wing helped to identify the *Staffelführer's* machine *(via VanWyngarden)*

Along with many other JG III Fokkers, Bolle's last D VII was turned over to the RAF at war's end, and is seen here at Nivelles in December 1918. A later model than Bolle's other D VII, this one also had the fuselage decorated in black, white and yellow, and had two white stripes on the top wing. When this and other *Jasta* Boelcke aeroplanes were reluctantly handed over to the British after the Armistice, they were first inscribed with the number of Allied machines that each aircraft had destroyed *(via VanWyngarden)*

formation in August 1916. It had seen a lean time in the summer of 1917, but more than made up for this during the summer of 1918.

Karl Bolle had taken command as JG III was formed, and apart from some leave, he would lead it until the Armistice. Like his *Kommandeur*, Bolle was Berlin-born, on 20 June 1893, and in 1912 had studied economics at Oxford University, where his sporting prowess had also shone through. With the coming of war Bolle was with a Kurassier regiment, and he saw action in France, Poland and Courland, before transferring to the flying services in 1915. By July 1916 he was flying with *Kampfgeschwader* 4, where one of his observers was Lothar von Richthofen. Bolle was wounded in October and upon his return to duty was assigned to *Jasta* 28w in the summer of 1917.

His first victory was a British DH 4 bomber, and by the time he was given command of *Jasta* 2, he had achieved a total of five kills. Soldiering on with Albatros and Fokker Dr Is, Bolle's score rose to 20 on 5 July 1918, just as the D VIIs were starting to arrive in small numbers. Victory

A *Jasta* Boelcke mechanic poses proudly with his machine. The late historian A E Ferko tentatively identified this BMW-engined D VII (F) as possibly the machine of Ltn Otto Löffler, another extremely successful pilot in 1918. This photo was originally captioned 'With this machine I shot down ten aircraft', and circumstances point to Löffler as the author. All the visible markings on this D VII were probably black and white. The engine cowling aft of the white unit marking may have been black as well, and four-colour fabric covers the fuselage *(HAC/UTD via VanWyngarden)*

No 30 came on 11 August, when he downed a SPAD over the Amiens battle front, followed on the 26th by an American Camel from the 17th Aero Squadron – one of two US Camel squadrons attached to the British 65th Wing. In fact both Squadrons, the 17th and 148th were in action with JG III this day, the opening day of the Battle of the Scarpe, and they took a beating. The 17th lost six pilots to JG III and the 148th one. Despite claims by the Americans, the *Geschwader* had no pilot losses. *Jasta* Boelcke scored two of the victories and *Jasta* 27 got four, while Loerzer may have been responsible for shooting down ace 2Lt R M Todd.

Bolle's scoring rate then fell off somewhat. He only gained one more in August, but on the 28th of that month came his *Pour le Mérite*. For the first half of September he was on leave, but he did not score another kill until 1 November, followed by three on 4 November, two of which were Sopwith Snipes of No 4 Sqn AFC. Two of the three Snipes which fell that day were flown by aces, Capt T C R Baker DFC MM (12 victories) and Lt A J Palliser (seven victories).

Bolle remained associated with aviation post-war, and in the early 1920s he was appointed Director of the German Transportation Flying School, and later was in charge of all pilot training. He became a special advisor to the Luftwaffe in the 1930s, reporting to Hermann Göring. He died in his native Berlin on 9 October 1955.

The pilot who took temporary command of the Boelcke *Staffel* in September was Ltn Otto Löffler, who was also to score heavily in the D VII. A former grenadier until he moved into aviation, he joined *Jasta* Boelcke in the late autumn of 1917, shooting down his first enemy on 5 December. By the time the *Jasta* became part of JG III, Löffler had downed another, but then did not score again until after the D VII had arrived – in fact, the first day of the Amiens battle, on 9 August. In the meantime he had himself been shot down twice, once force-landing in 'no-man's land' just a few metres from the British trenches. A French bomber on 21 August

The striped *Jasta* Boelcke D VII (OAW) 4453/18 of Ltn Alfred Lindenberger provides a fine setting for this portrait. Lindenberger scored perhaps his last eight of 12 World War 1 victories in D VIIs. He had earlier scored his first three victories in Fl. Abt. (A) 234, and was awarded Württemberg's Gold Military Merit Medal. The striping on his D VII may have been inspired by the yellow and black ribbon of this medal. Lindenberger flew in the Luftwaffe in World War 2, and scored an additional four victories in that conflict *(A Imrie via HAC/UTD)*

Lindenberger's D VII (OAW) 4453/18 was also interned at Nivelles after the war, and it shows up in many photos. Here it is the foremost machine, with the tail of an Albatros D Va to the left. The tail section of Lindenberger's D VII is divided in the half black/half white marking of *Jasta* Boelcke. The third D VII in the line is *Jasta* 26 machine 501/18 *(via VanWyngarden)*

The most successful *Jasta* Boelcke pilot was the redoubtable Paul Bäumer, who was finally commissioned in April 1918. He returned to *Jasta* Boelcke in September of that year following a long convalescence after being injured in a serious crash, and began a meteoric scoring streak, raising his tally from 21 to 43 in little more than a month. He was shot down in this same month but was luckily saved by his parachute, and received the *Pour le Mérite* only nine days before the Armistice *(HAC/UTD via VanWyngarden)*

provided him with kill number four, and then he seemed to get 'his eye in' for during September he brought his score to 13, with two more in October.

In World War 2 Löffler's son Kurt was a fighter pilot, and he also became an ace with 26 victories, 15 whilst flying with JG 51.

Alfred Lindenberger of *Jasta* 2 was also associated with World War 2, but as a fighter pilot himself. He started his First War flying in the usual fashion, via two-seaters in 1917 as an observer. His first three victories were shared with his pilots, two with ace Kurt Jentsch. Following pilot training, Lindenberger was sent to *Jasta* Boelcke in May 1918, and had gained victory number four before that month was out. The fifth came on 1 June, and his next seven kills were scored flying a D VII between 18 August and 1 November.

He joined the Luftwaffe in the inter-war years, and with the rank of major saw action as a fighter pilot again late in that war. Lindenberger was flying with JG 3 in June 1944 and then II.*Gruppe* of JG 300 in Home Defence duties – from October 1944 through to February 1945 he commanded JG 300 in its entirety. During September 1944 this veteran ace scored four kills against American aircraft – three four-engined bombers and one P-51 Mustang.

By far the most exciting fighter pilot with *Jasta* Boelcke was Ltn Paul Bäumer, who was born in Duisberg-Ruhrart on 22 May 1896. He paid for private flying lessons pre-war whilst working as a dentist's assistant, and had his licence by the summer of 1914. Despite this, his early military career when war came was with the German infantry – he fought in France and Russia, where he was wounded in the left arm. Managing to transfer to the air service as a dental assistant, he was then able to request pilot training. No doubt due to his previous flying experience, once fully trained Bäumer was retained as an instructor and ferry pilot in the autumn of 1916, but finally, in early 1917 he went to a two-seater unit as a gefreiter, then promoted to unteroffizier.

Bäumer got onto fighters in June, going to *Jasta* 5, where he claimed three victories in July – all kite balloons – and then moved to *Jasta* Boelcke in August. By the end of the year he had 18 victories, No 19 coming in March 1918, then a commission on 10 April, with his score at 22. His 20th kill on 23 March was *Jasta* Boelcke's 200th victory. Bäumer did not score again before breaking his jaw in a crash, apparently whilst flying in a Pfalz D VIII, on 29 May. He returned to the *Jasta* in September. There had been no sign of a *Pour le Mérite*, meantime, despite his score of 22, but this may have spurred him on.

With the BMW-engined Fokker D VII, Bäumer fairly ripped into the RAF in September. By the 20th his tally was 27, then he scored in multiples – three on the 21st, two on the 24th and three more on both the 27th and 29th, bringing his total to 39. Bäumer was also shot down himself during the month, but was saved by his parachute. However, following his 30th victory he was finally recommended for the 'Blue Max', which he received nine days before the Armistice. By this time, with a further five victories in early October, his war total of victories had reached 43. All Bäumer's victories had been scored against the RFC/RAF with the exception of one American Camel.

Post-war he worked briefly for Blohm und Voss aeroplane manufacturers situated in Hamburg docks, but finally became a professional dentist. This did not detract from his interest in flying, first as an aerobatic pilot and then as an aeroplane builder with his own Bäumer Aero GmbH company in Hamburg. However, during an aeroplane display at Copenhagen, test flying a Rohrbach Rofix fighter, he crashed two kilometres from the coast of the Oere Sound on 15 July 1927 and was killed.

Gerhard Bassenge was yet another infantryman turned aviator. From Ettlingen, where he was born on 18 November 1897, he was commissioned in the field in January 1915. Transferred to the Air Service on 1 April 1916, Bassenge completed his pilot training and then served with *Kampfstaffel* 39, before going to *Jasta* 5 in April 1917.

At the start of May he moved to *Jasta* Boelcke, but did not gain his first combat victory until 20 October – a Sopwith Camel. Less than a month later he had downed another Camel. On 6 November 1917 Bassenge was wounded by anti-aircraft shrapnel, but returned to *Jasta* Boelcke several months later. By the time he scored again on 25 July 1918, the D VII was starting to arrive and his last four victories were all gained on this type. Most of his victims were fighters, including at least four Camels and possibly two SE 5as – he is generally credited with six or seven victories.

Bassenge served in the army after the war while studying engineering. Promoted to captain in 1932 and major in 1935, he commanded the parachute school at Stendal as an oberstleutnant from April 1937, and in World War 2 served in the Luftwaffe in Rumania and North Africa. Captured as Axis forces collapsed in Tunisia, on 10 May 1943, Bassenge remained as prisoner until 1947. He died in Lübeck on 13 March 1977.

Ernst Bormann, from Kirchbreck, near Holzminden, joined up as an officer cadet in August 1915. This 17-year-old, born on 5 November 1897, then transferred from his reserve infantry regiment to the air service, and by early 1918 he had become a two-seater pilot. Moving on to fighters he was sent to Jasta *Boelcke* on 4 May.

Bormann was to remain with this unit until the end of the war, and he would rack up 16 victories between 3 July and 4 November 1918,

A relaxed Paul Bäumer is captured in conversation with a non-flying NCO member of *Jasta* Boelcke, as well as a canine friend. The *Jasta* Boelcke D VII had an overpainted fuselage, and a coloured band with white edging. Like so many other German fighter pilots, Bäumer had flown the Albatros D V and Fokker Dr I with some success, but his scoring rate really blossomed once he acquired the BMW-engined Fokker D VII (F) *(via VanWyngarden)*

A line-up of splendidly decorated D VIIs of *Jasta* Boelcke at Aniche aerodrome, occupied by the unit in November 1918 *(via VanWyngarden)*

including three Camels of the 148th US Aero Squadron on the afternoon of 2 September. His final victory was a No 4 Sqn AFC Snipe, one of three he and his *Staffelführer* Karl Bolle shot down, which included two aces. At least 14 of his 16 kills were probably achieved in the D VII.

Between August 1925 and September 1930 Bormann was a flight instructor at Lizak, in Russia, and again in Germany post-1930. He joined the Luftwaffe as a captain in 1934, and between 1935 and 1938 was a *Staffelkäpitan* with KG *Boelcke*. He had a distinguished World War 2 career, and by June 1943 was a major-general.

Bormann was captured by victorious Russian forces on 10 May 1945 and was destined to remain a prisoner until October 1955. After his release he received a Doctorate, and died in Düsseldorf on 1 August 1960.

JASTA 26

Bruno Loerzer had been the first leader of *Jasta* 26 following its formation in late 1916. When he was given command of JG III in February 1918, his younger brother Fritz took over, transferring in from *Jasta* 63. Despite his 12 victories, Fritz was shot down and taken prisoner on 12 June 1918, apparently in one of the first D VIIs to be used by the *Jasta*. The Fokkers of this veteran *Staffel* would bear the unit's traditional broad black/white bands on their fuselages and tails.

Ltn Franz Brandt was the next commanding officer, arriving on 28 June as acting CO, until confirmed in the job on 2 July. Brandt came from Minden, born on 13 February 1893, and in August 1914 was with an artillery regiment. Transferred into aviation in July 1915 he flew with KG 3 the following year, then with a *Schutzstaffel* in December. Arriving at *Jasta* 19 in February 1917, he gained two kills before moving to *Jasta* 27, where he brought his score to five, and then came to *Jasta* 26 as CO.

Brandt's final war victory score was ten, with at least three more unconfirmed. Apart from one balloon, all but two of these successes were over fighters, including a Nieuport 28 from the 94th Aero Squadron. He survived the war.

Vzfw Erich Buder had served with *Jasta* 5 before moving to Jasta 26 on 25 January 1918, but had no victories at this date. However, his first came on 26 March during Operation *Michael*, and by early July he had three. Now flying the D VII, Buder scored 12 confirmed kills, with two more unconfirmed, by war's end, these being a variety of British, French and American machines.

Another notable NCO pilot with *Jasta* 26 in the summer of 1918 was Vzfw Fritz Classen. He learnt to fly in 1915, and his first unit was a two-seater reconnaissance *abteilung*. Classen and one of his observers claimed a victory over a British Nieuport Scout on 24 July 1917, and not long afterwards he moved to *Jasta* 3, in January 1918. 13 February saw a move to *Jasta* 26, and by the time Fokker biplanes were arriving, Classen had four victories

Visiting German nurses take a close look at one of *Jasta* 26's D VIIs whilst being entertained by the unit's pilots in the summer of 1918. This Fokker-built machine displays the *Staffel* markings of broad black/white bands on the fuselage and tailplane, and its unidentified pilot has personalised his aircraft with a '5', marked on a dirty white (or coloured) band aft of the cockpit. In common with many other machines from JG III, this personal marking was repeated on the centre section of the upper wing, taking the form of a white '5' on the four-colour fabric *(via VanWyngarden)*

Much the worse for wear, this highly decorated Fokker-built D VII was photographed in Allied hands post-war, probably at Nivelles in Belgium. Although considerably worn, it obviously displays the black and white markings of *Jasta* 26, including a black-outlined rudder. The black/white stripes on the underside of the lower wing suggest that it was flown by a formation leader, and was possibly another of Bruno Loerzer's aircraft – or perhaps the CO of the *Staffel*, Ltn d R Franz Brandt? The uppersurface of the top wing was also striped, but possibly in colours other than black and white *(via VanWyngarden)*

to his name. Between 27 August and 30 October he shot down seven more aircraft, making 11 in total, plus three unconfirmed.

A third NCO ace was Vzfw Christian Mesch. It is uncertain if he gained his first victory prior to joining *Jasta* 26, or if an initially unconfirmed victory on 15 July 1918 was later confirmed, but in any event he was credited with 13 kills by 26 September. Mesch had three claims by the time of the arrival of the D VIIs, so nine or ten were scored with the Fokker biplane fighter. His victory on 5 September was over a Camel flown by the 12-kill Australian ace Lt L T E Taplin DFC of No 4 Sqn AFC, who was brought down and taken prisoner. Upon his return from prison camp Taplin recorded;

'The formation went over the line in V-formation. We were flying at about 14,000 ft and our escort could not be seen – I did not like the situation and climbed another 1000 ft above the patrol. Soon after this, in the region of Douai, we were attacked. There were three formations in the attacking enemy, all Fokker biplanes. Two formations of about 12 to 15 machines attacked almost simultaneously, one from high up in the west and one from the north. Later, a very much larger formation came in from the east, which I first thought was our escort coming to our rescue.

'The leader – a red and white tailed Fokker – pulled up and we went at it head-on. I got a good burst into his radiator and he went down in a glide – not out of control – just engine out of action. Next moment I was right in the middle of them, and before I could do anything a German below me pulled his nose up and put a burst right through the bottom of my machine. One bullet went through my right hand, smashing it up and breaking my wrist. My Camel immediately stalled and half rolled itself, and to conform with poetic justice, came out of the stall right on the tail of my attacker, who was recovering from his own stall. I was now under control with my left hand and easily shot this German down.

'I was getting shot about and firing at anything I saw when a Fokker from somewhere again got a burst into me. One bullet – an explosive – smashed the breach and crank-handle of one of my guns and sent a splinter through my nose. This dazed me and I fell out of control in an engine-spin. I spun down to about 1000 ft and then recovered to find two Fokkers had followed me down. I again had to fight, and luckily shot one down easily – the other then left me alone.'

Taplin, now down to 100 ft or so, headed for the lines, but he then said he was finished off by German ground fire and had to crash land just short of the Allied trenches. Whether or not Mesch had seen him head away and then crash is not known, but when the victory credits were assessed, this Camel was noted as being the one he had shot down. However, it could just as easily have been Vzfw Lux of *Jasta* 27 who got him (see later) or in fact any of the German claimants in what had developed into a complex air fight.

Helmut Lange scored his first victory with *Jasta* 26 on 26 March 1918, with two more following in May. His next victory, on 27 August, was after the unit had re-equipped with D VIIs. Between 26 August and 12 September, he was acting commander, and by the end of the war Lange's score had risen to nine – six single-seat fighters, two BE 2b fighters and one DH 9 bomber.

The star of *Jasta* 26 was, of course, Otto Fruhner, who became another top ace whom fate denied the 'Blue Max'. Born in Brieg on 6 September 1893, his service with the air service had begun as a mechanic in November 1914, but the following year he managed a transfer to pilot training and by May 1916 was flying two-seaters on the Eastern Front. Promoted to unteroffizier in August, Fruhner volunteered for fighters the following year and finally joined Loerzer's *Jasta* 26 in July as a vizefeldwebel.

His first two victories came on 3 September 1917, but he had to wait until 3 January 1918 for his third. However, by the end of January Fruhner's score had doubled, and by the end of March this had become six. As with so many others, he really began to score once the D VIIs arrived, and by 20 September his score had reached 27 – the vast majority of which were single-seat fighters. In fact only four were two-seaters, and one of those a BE 2b. On 4 September, two days before his 25th birthday, Fruhner shot down three Camels of No 70 Sqn.

Twelve Camels from this outfit had encountered the Fokkers of JG III that day, and the *geschwader* inflicted the single biggest loss of fighters the RAF suffered in a single fight in World War 1. Canadian Lt Ken Watson, one of the four survivors from the British squadron, later reported;

'While on OP (Offensive Patrol) at 0815 hrs over Escaillon, the patrol dived on 15 Fokker biplanes and a further 15 Fokkers dived on the patrol, coming out of the clouds from 12,000 ft. I saw one EA (Enemy Aircraft) on Lt Gower's tail. I engaged him at close range and shot him down in flames.'

Although eight Camels failed to return, JG III pilots claimed 11 in all – seven to *Jasta* 26, one to *Jasta* 27, two to JG III's adjutant Dahlmann and one to Bruno Loerzer. Friedrich Noltenius of *Jasta* 27 missed out, for although he felt certain he had inflicted 'serious hurt' on one of the Camels, it was finally credited to another pilot (see later).

Significantly, several of JG III's Fokkers had the new BMW engines, and the Camels of No 70 Sqn were still Clerget-engined powered. The latter had 20 less horsepower than the Bentley-engined Camels, so were at a disadvantage anyway.

Fruhner was commissioned by this time, but his luck ran out on 20 September when he collided with a Camel of No 203 Sqn. Although this was credited as his 27th victory, he was injured and had to take to his parachute, which functioned normally and brought him safely down to earth. This incident ended his war flying, and although nominated for the *Pour le Mérite*,

Hermann Göring, as commander of *Jasta* 27, briefs his pilots in front of one of his white-nosed Fokker Dr Is on Iseghem aerodrome, circa June 1918. The early-production D VII at the extreme left is also believed to have been one of Göring's machines (possibly 278/18 or 324/18). While most *Jasta* 27 Fokkers bore yellow noses, tails and struts, Göring's aircraft had these components painted white to distinguish the *Staffelführer's* mount. The wheel covers were white as well *(via VanWyngarden)*

This photo from the Göring albums certainly shows one of his *Jagdstaffel* 27 Fokkers, perhaps 278/18. It clearly displays the white nose, struts and wheel covers which helped identify the commander's D VII. Göring scored his 21st victory in 278/18 on 17 June 1918 – a SPAD which fell into the forest west of Ambleny heights. In his combat report from that flight he also confirmed another SPAD downed by Ltn Brandt, and described the fatal collision between two other Fokkers from his unit (Oblt von Förster and Vzfw Wilhelm Schäfer) *(via VanWyngarden)*

Seen here with his *Jasta* Boelcke Dr I, Hermann Frommherz scored the lion's share of his 32 victories flying the D VII. In fact, after being appointed commander of *Jasta* 27 following Göring's transfer to JG I, Frommherz more than tripled his score in just over three months *(via VanWyngarden)*

this had not been approved by the time of the Kaiser's abdication.

In 1935 Fruhner joined the Luftwaffe with the rank of major and commanded the flying school at Ludwigslust, and during World War 2 remained in various training schools and commands, eventually reaching the rank of major-general. He died in Villach, southern Bavaria, on 19 June 1965.

Mention of JG III's adjutant in the action on 4 September 1918 is appropriate when dealing with *Jasta* 26, for Dahlmann had been with this unit prior to becoming adjutant, and generally flew a D VII in *Staffel* colours with the unit when his duties allowed.

Oblt Theodor Hermann Dahlmann, usually known as Hermann, was born on 19 November 1892 in Wanfried, Hessen. He had joined the army in the spring of 1913, serving as an infantry officer before transferring to aviation in July 1915. Between May and October 1916 he had served with a two-seater *abteilung*, before going over to single-seaters in March 1917.

Dahlmann's first unit had been *Jasta* 29 from 15 April, with whom he achieved one victory – a kite balloon – downed on 1 June. Promoted to oberleutant in January 1918, whilst commanding a training school, he was posted to *Jasta* 26 once it had become part of JG III, in July. Between 14 August and 29 October he claimed six victories on D VIIs to bring his score to seven.

In World War 2 Dahlmann rose to the rank of general in the Luftwaffe, serving in the German Air Ministry. He died on 21 January 1978 at the age of 85.

JASTA 27

Hermann Göring was still commanding *Jasta* 27 upon the formation of JG III, and continued to do so until he went to JG I in July 1918. Towards the end of his tenure as *Staffelführer*, he downed victories 20 and 21 whilst flying the new D VII, on 9 and 17 June respectively, and with his single kill with JG I on 18 July, this gave him just three kills on the type.

The new leader of *Staffel* 27 was Hermann Frommherz, who had already reached ace status with *Jasta* Boelcke in 1917 and in the early summer of 1918. Frommherz came from Waldshut, Baden, a town near the Swiss border, where he was born on 10 August 1891. He became an engineering student in Stuttgart, and in late 1911 joined a *Jäger* regiment within the army reserve. At the start of the war Frommherz saw service in France as a vizefeldwebel, prior to moving to an infantry unit and then seeing action on the Russian front. Transferred to aviation at the start of June 1915, his first unit was *Kampfstaffel* 20 of KG 4. Commissioned in August 1916, Frommherz went to Macedonia and Salonika with KG 1.

With an impressive amount of experience thus far, he became a fighter pilot in March 1917 and scored two victories, but was injured in a crash

Arguably one of the most skilful of all D VII aces was Ltn d R Friedrich Noltenius, who scored at least 21 confirmed victories (along with several unconfirmed claims) in just over four months. He flew in *Jagdstaffeln* 27, 6 and 11, and his thoughtful and revealing diary provides one of the best descriptions available of flying the formidable D VII in the *Geschwader* combats of 1918 *(HAC/UTD)*

Friedrich Noltenius (with walking stick) and his visiting brother Armin strike a relaxed pose with Noltenius' D VII (OAW) of *Jasta* 27. The nose does not seem to bear the yellow finish which characterised *Staffel* 27 aircraft, but the tailplane may well have been yellow. The pilot's personal markings were the red and white stripes on the fuselage and upper wing, these colours being emblematic of Noltenius' native Bremen and the Hanseatic League. The fuselage has been described as 'grey', but it was most probably simply four-colour fabric dulled by over varnishing *(via VanWyngarden)*

on 1 May. Recovering, he became an instructor for a while, returning to *Jasta* Boelcke on 1 March 1918. By the end of July 1918 Frommherz had scored a total of ten victories, and thus became acting leader of *Jasta* 27.

He began his run of successes on 9 August – two days after his position had been confirmed – during the early stage of the Battle of Amiens, and gained his 13th, 14th and 15th kills in that fight against the Americans of the 17th and 148th Aero Squadrons on 26 August. September saw Frommherz run his score to 26, the last two of which were SE 5as from No 40 Sqn, and by the end of the war his total had reached 32. According to *Jasta* 27 pilot Ernst de Ritter, Frommherz flew a gaudy Fokker marked with the unit's yellow nose and tail markings, and red and black chevron-pattern stripes on the upper wing to identify him as *Staffelführer*.

Frommherz had received a chest-full of decorations by this time, and although nominated for the *Pour le Mérite*, the Armistice came before it was ratified. He obviously thought he deserved to receive it for some post-war photos of him show him wearing the medal.

Frommherz remained active in aviation post-war, firstly with the German Police Aviation Service, then as a mail pilot with the Deutsche-Luftreederie, which later became the German airline Lufthansa. He returned to his native Baden in 1920 as technical chief at a new airfield at Lorrach, but with the severe flying restrictions placed on Germany, he went to Russia in 1925, and then to China between 1931-32, teaching Chiang Kai-shek's new air force pilots fighter tactics. Back in Germany for World War 2, Frommherz commanded I *Gruppe* of JG 134, and later rose to generalmajor. He returned to civic affairs in his home-town of Waldshut at the end of the war, where he died on 30 December 1964 following a heart attack.

The son of a Professor of Medicine, Friedrich Theodor Noltenius was born in Bremen on 8 January 1894. He himself had plans to become a doctor, but these were cut short with the outbreak of war in 1914, in which he initially enlisted into the artillery. For a year he served on the Eastern Front, then France, where Noltenius continued to see action until November 1917. Having been commissioned in October 1916, wounded in April 1917 and then decorated, he transferred into aviation at the end of that year.

After becoming a pilot, his period on two-seaters was brief, and in mid-July 1918 Noltenius was posted to *Jasta* 27. At the start of the Amiens Offensive in August he shot down his first British aircraft, followed by two more and a balloon before that month was out. He

Noltenius of *Jasta* 27 survived a harrowing attack on a British balloon on 14 September. When he was a mere 50 metres away from the balloon, it erupted in flames and he was forced to fly through the explosion. Noltenius later wrote, 'the machine was still in flying condition, but what a shambles she was! The cloth covering had become completely slack all over the machine and billowed'. Visible in this photo are shreds of balloon cloth entangled in the cabane struts. Noltenius was still able to fly the sturdy D VII home and make a safe landing, but the Fokker was a write-off, and he duly took over Fw Willy Kahle's aircraft

This damaged JG III Fokker may be the aircraft Friedrich Noltenius was flying on 22 September when, during a scrap with some Sopwiths, 'the cloth covering of the top wing had torn off and several ribs were broken in the hectic dogfight'. This was one of several D VII structural problems Noltenius experienced, but survived. The Bristol F 2B in the right, marked 'K', was E2514 of No 22 Sqn, which had been brought down by Frommherz on 27 August 1918 *(via VanWyngarden)*

gained two victories on 2 September, but in a later flight that day he almost shot himself down! He later wrote;

'Another sortie was flown that evening. We began to dive on some Sopwiths. I quickly closed in to shooting range, fired, and suddenly was jolted by a mighty shock – water from the radiator and petrol vapour splashed into my face. I made a sharp turn, broke away and unfastened my belts because I expected the crate to start burning at any moment. I could not see anything, and only flew away from the front as a first measure as we had been deep in enemy territory. I had a hell of a time getting the machine back to our field. The engine quit while I was still taxiing. What had happened? The cowling panels had been torn loose by the slipstream and blocked off the gun muzzles. This had deflected my own bullets into the radiator and the intake manifold!'

By the end of September Noltenius' score stood at 13, although he noted that he had lost a few kills to other pilots, notably on 4 September, on the occasion of the massacre of No 70 Sqn. He wrote in his diary;

'After a while a lively aerial battle with a strong Sopwith squadron commenced. I tried hard to get higher up in order to catch one of them, if possible, when he attempted to fly back to his lines. I was successful in this – I caught one and spiralled downward with him to 300 metres. Then a section of my top wing broke off – the part aft of the second main spar – and I had to give up.

'The Sopwith later landed in a normal manner. In the course of the fight another Sopwith came to the assistance of the first one. I evaded him

Rudolf Klimke's *Jasta* 27 D VII appears indistinctly in the background of this serious portrait of the 17-victory ace. This Fokker-built machine was marked with broad white-bordered black chevron stripes on the top wing. The tail, nose and struts were probably *Jasta* 27 yellow, and a similar yellow(?) band is seen aft of the cockpit. It is possible Klimke's personal talisman of a black anchor was also painted on this coloured band *(via VanWyngarden)*

and continued to pursue the first opponent. The plane was later shot down by Lux. Fruhner also claimed this one. The decision had not yet been made, but it will no doubt be like this – Lux one, Fruhner the other.'

During October Noltenius, having moved to *Jasta* 6 and then *Jasta* 11, accounted for six further victories, including two balloons and a SPAD on the 23rd. In all he claimed eight balloons in his final tally of 21 victories, that total being reached with two DH 4 bombers downed on 3 and 4 November. These were achieved during 141 operational sorties. One of his unconfirmed claims was a Camel on 21 September, which went down on the British side of the lines, and is believed to have been flown by Capt W R May of No 209 Sqn, who was unhurt. It had been May who had been pursued over Australian lines on 21 April by Manfred von Richthofen, a flight from which the Rittmeister did not return.

Noltenius received the Knight's Cross of the Hohenzollern House Order on 8 November, a decoration normally the prerequisite for the nomination of the 'Blue Max', but as the war ended three days later, no action was taken on the latter. After the war he flew against the communists, but finally he was allowed to return to his medical studies to become a doctor. He and his family lived in South America from 1922 to 1933, and with the approach of World War 2 Noltenius returned to the homeland, where he took up flying once more. On 12 March 1936 he crashed taking off from Johannistal Airport in a Bücker Jungmann and died on his way to hospital. Noltenius was 42.

Albert Lux reached *Jasta* 27 in November 1917, but it was not until 1 April 1918 that he gained his first combat victory. His second kill came on 9 August, by which time Fokker biplanes had arrived, and from then until the end of the war he shot down a total of eight British aircraft – six fighters and two two-seaters.

Another *Jasta* 27 pilot with a vast amount of experience and service was Ltn Rudolf Klimke. He was also lucky to survive the war. Born on 8 November 1890, at Merseberg, he had been with the artillery from late 1910 and had joined the flying service in August 1915. Flying two-seaters with various units in France and Russia, Klimke had been credited with one victory in Russia in September 1916.

In May 1917, now an offizierstellvertreter, he and his observer flew a lone night bombing raid on London in an Albatros CV II from their base near Ostende. Moving to KG 3 to fly large Gotha bombers, Klimke and his crew claimed a victory over a Sopwith during another London raid on 7 July. It was not long after this that he was posted to *Jasta* 27 as a fighter pilot, and by the end of the year he had five victories in total.

By the early summer of 1918 Klimke's score had risen to eight as the unit began to equip with the D VII. During August he added seven more to his tally, and two more in the first half of September made it 17 in total. Wounded in his last combat by three bullets in the shoulder during a fight with a Bristol F 2B Fighter, Klimke landed back at base safely but was nearly killed when the hospital he was recuperating in was hit during a bombing raid.

His personal insignia on his Dr I was a black anchor on the fuselage, repeated on the elevators. Ernst de Ritter later recorded that Klimke had always encouraged others to attack more and more, but when he visited the wounded ace in hospital he told de Ritter to 'be careful'!

Wilhelm Neuenhofen was to become a 15-victory ace with *Jasta* 27, between 9 June and the Armistice. Born on 24 April 1897 in München Gladbach, he joined the German air service on 1 July 1915 and served as an NCO in FA(A) 215 during the second half of 1917 on the Russian Front. Becoming a fighter pilot, Neuenhofen joined *Jasta* 27 as a vizefeldwebel in early 1918, but did not make a successful claim until he downed a SPAD on 9 June.

With the arrival of the D VII he really got into his stride, and by 29 September, on which date he was commissioned, he had achieved nine kills. In October Neuenhofen added four more, and with two kills on 4 November, his score had reached 15. One of his victories, on 22 September, was over a Camel flown by the American George A Vaughn Jr of the 17th Aero Squadron, who had taken his score to nine that same day. He survived being shot down to achieve a total of 13 kills by war's end.

After the war Neuenhofen remained in aviation, and was eventually killed in an aeroplane accident on 24 January 1936 at the Junkers Aircraft Company airfield at Dessau.

JASTA 36

There were four aces in *Jasta* 36 who may have achieved some victories in the D VII – Harry von Bülow, Theodor Quandt, Alfred Hübner and Kurt Jacob. *Staffel* 36 seems to have received D VIIs later than the other component units of JG III, and as late as 17 September 1918 it had a mixed bag of Dr Is, some E V parasols and D VIIs. The unit marking was a blue nose.

Von Bülow, or to give him his full title, Harry von Bülow-Bothkamp, he was the younger brother of Walter von Bülow, the 28-victory ace who had previously commanded this same *Jagdstaffel* during the second half of 1917. Winner of the *Pour le Mérite,* Walter had been killed in action on 6 January 1918, by which time Harry had scored three kills himself. He claimed three more in 1918, the last two on the D VII, but then, as the only surviving son of the three Bothkamp brothers from Holstein, he was taken out of frontline service.

Harry had been born at Bothkamp Castle on 19 November 1897, and following service with a Saxon Hussar regiment, learnt to fly in 1916. He spent time with two two-seater units until he was posted to his brother's *Jasta*. His last victory had been over the CO of No 73 Sqn, Maj R N Freeman, who was flying a Camel.

During World War 2 von Bülow was CO of II *Gruppe* of JG 77, commanded JG 2 'Richthofen' and later led nightfighter *Gruppen* NJG 101 and NJG 105. He was reputed to have scored victories in the early days of World War 2, and received the Knight's Cross of the Iron Cross on 22 August 1940 as an oberstleutnant. He commanded the 5th Fighter Division in 1943. Surviving his second war, von Bülow died at Bothkamp Castle on 27 February 1976.

Theo Quandt was the same age as Harry von Bülow, although five months his senior, having been born on 22 June 1897 in Molland, East Prussia. He became a professional army infantry officer and was on active service as soon as the war began. Quandt saw action on the Eastern Front and then in the West, before joining the air service in July 1915. He became a two-seater pilot at the start of 1917, then moved to *Jasta* 36 at

A portion of the command staff of the short-lived Bavarian JG IV, all of whom wear Heinecke parachute harnesses. They are, from left to right, Ltn d R Alfred Freytag (JG IV Adjutant), Ltn d R Rudolf Stark (*Jasta* 35b commander, 11 victories), Oblt Eduard von Schleich (JG IV commander, 35 victories) and Ltn Heinrich Seywald (*Jasta* 23b commander, six victories). Both Schleich and Stark wear captured British 'Sidcot' flying suits, which were highly prized by German airmen *(via VanWyngarden)*

Christmas 1917. After gaining eight victories, he was given command of *Jasta* 53, but did not score with this unit, and then in August 1918 returned to command *Jasta* 36. Two victories in August and five more in September brought Quandt's score to 15, the last seven perhaps being scored on the D VII.

His 11th victory on 1 September 1918 had been an SE 5a of No 84 Sqn, flown by American ace Capt J O Donaldson DFC, who was taken prisoner, although he escaped later. Quandt's final seven victories were over Allied fighters – three Camels, three SE 5as and a Bristol Fighter.

Like von Bülow, Quandt too served in fighters during early World War 2, as a major, but he was shot down and killed on 6 June 1940 by French fighters whilst flying a Bf 109E with JG 3 during the Battle of France.

Vzfw Alfred Hübner came from Lauenberg, where he was born on 26 October 1891. He served as a gefreiter in the Army from October 1912, seeing action in the infantry and rising to unteroffizier by the time he moved into aviation during September 1915. After flying two-seaters Hübner was sent to *Jasta* 36 in February 1918, and of his six victories, perhaps at least four were scored in a D VII. His final kill came on 30 October when he downed a Bristol Fighter of No 88 Sqn.

BAVARIAN *JAGDGESCHWADER* IV

Next to Prussia, the most powerful state in Imperial Germany was Bavaria. Indeed, Bavaria was operating its own air service at the start of the Great War, and by late 1918 had many of its own military formations within the German air service. Thus, perhaps somewhat belatedly, Royal Bavarian JG IV was formed on 3 October 1918 under the command of Hptm Eduard von Schleich (according to official *Flieger Formation* data, it was established on 10 October and confirmed by a *Bayerisches Kriegsministerium* order on the 28th). It was composed of four Bavarian *Staffeln* – 23b, 32b, 34b and 35b. The four component units assembled in the *Armee Abteilung* 'A' sector before being sent to the 2. *Armee* front.

Jasta 23b was commanded by Ltn Heinrich Seywald, already a six-victory ace, but he did not score again before war's end.

Jasta 32b was led by Emil Koch, a seven-victory ace, who likewise did not score again before being wounded on 24 October. His place was

The famous Bavarian fighter pilot Eduard Ritter von Schleich, later known popularly as the 'Black Knight', is seen here wearing a coveted British leather flying coat. He was appointed commander of *Jagdgruppe* 8b in March 1918, and eventually flew the D VII, probably obtaining approximately his last six (of 35) victories in the type. Schleich was named commander of Bavarian JG IV, but scored no more victories during the brief career of that formation *(via VanWyngarden)*

Oblt Robert Greim (later Ritter von Greim) was the *Jastaführer* of Bavarian *Jagdstaffel* 34 in 1918, and he is seen here with his D VII (Alb). His machine was identified by the silvery-white rear fuselage of the *Staffel* and Greim's own two red bands just aft of the cockpit. The fin and rudder were factory-finish white *(via VanWyngarden)*

This unique photo from the von Greim albums reveals his D VII (Alb) of *Jasta* 34b in full markings. The fuselage from the cockpit aft was the *Staffel* colour of silver/white, while Greim's two red bands have been retouched in to emphasise them. The rest of the machine retained its four-colour fabric finish – a tubular sight was fixed between the guns. The similarly-marked D VII in the background may have been Vzfw Pütz's machine, marked with two green bands. The six-victory pilot Vzfw Kahlow reportedly flew a machine with one yellow band, and Ltn d R Kröhl (four victories) used one red band *(P Kilduff via GVW)*

Jasta 35b leader Rudolf Stark was photographed with his newly-arrived D VII (OAW) 4523/18 circa August 1918. The nose still retains its OAW-style 'patch camouflage' in purple and green, although by this time the *Staffel* marking of a large chevron had been painted on the upper wing in Stark's own lilac colour. The serial number was stencilled on the wheel cover in white. This D VII was covered in four-colour fabric *(A Imrie via HAC/UTD)*

taken by Ltn Hans Böhning for the last 11 days of the war, and although an established ace with 17 kills, he did not add to this number either.

Jasta 34b had been led by Oblt Robert Greim since 19 June 1917, during which time he had commanded *Jagdgruppe* Nr 10 (also known as JGr Greim), in March-April 1918, and he was about to receive the 'Blue Max' for his 25 victories. Greim added three more victories to his tally while with JG IV – two SE 5as on 23 October and another on the 25th. However, he had begun flying his D VII (Alb) in June – well before JG IV was formed – and may have achieved around 14 victories in total on the type.

Together with one of his top pilots, Vzfw Johann Pütz (seven victories), Greim had repeatedly strafed a British tank on 23 August 1918. After the war he would receive credit for its destruction in order to qualify him for the Knight's Cross of the Military Max-Joseph Order, making him Robert Ritter von Greim.

The fourth unit, *Jasta* 35b, was commanded by Ltn Rudolf Stark, whose final victory score has always been confused due to his book *Wings of War*, published in 1933, and which has been in print virtually ever since. By this stage of the war the German Army was being pushed back, and although there was still much fighting in the air, victories were becoming fewer. Stark's only kill with JG IV came on 9 November – a No 56 Sqn SE 5a – which is believed to have been his 11th kill. He recorded;

'When about to turn homeward, I sight seven English scouts over Bavai Wood (near Maubeuge), flying lower than us and in a south-westerly direction. They are SE 5s. As they are directly over the dark wood, their ochre wings stand out in sharp contrast from the ground below. Their cockades shine like gaudy butterflies above the dark-brown background of dead foliage.

'We dive straight down on to these English machines. They are flying straight home, having apparently failed to notice us. I get the hindmost of them into my

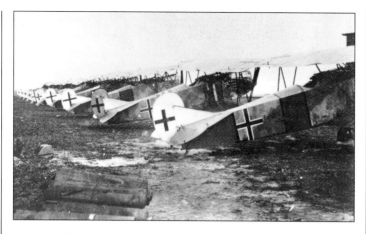

Six OAW-built D VIIs and four Pfalz D XIIs of *Jasta* 35b were on parade on Lieu St Amand field on 14 September 1918, carefully posed for an inspection by Gen von Bruck. The first machine on the right is Stark's 4523/18. At this stage it bore a lilac tail and band behind the cockpit, both edged in black. Portions of Stark's lilac chevron are visible on the top wing. The second aircraft is Gefr Prey's with black/white bands, next is Gefr Schmidt's with a dark red band and the fourth was Ltn Stoer's D VII with a green band bearing a white 'H' *(A Imrie via HAC/UTD)*

sights and fire several bursts. At last it heels over and goes down in a spin, falling into the wood, where it is caught by the mass of branches.'

The RAF squadron made no comment on this loss, so Stark must have picked off the SE 5a without anyone seeing him fall.

With the war virtually over, JG IV had little opportunity to score victories before the Armistice. In fact *Jasta* 23b claimed only two, both falling to Uffz Michael Hutterer for his seventh and eighth kills. However, the seventh was a British Camel ace, Lt A Buchanan DFC of No 210 Sqn on 30 October, who became a prisoner.

Jasta 32b also claimed just two victories with JG IV, while *Jasta* 34b got six – Greim's three, and Ltn Alfons Scheicher, acting CO while the former was acting leader of the *Jagdgeschwader*, got a Camel on 27 October to bring his personal score to six. *Jasta* 35b's sole victory within JG IV was Stark's 9 November victory.

The finale for *Jasta* 35b. Fifteen glum fighter pilots were photographed on 11 November 1918 at Gosselies airfield as they sadly prepared to fly their Fokkers and Pfalz home to Germany. The pilots are, from left to right, Waldberer, Hensel, Werneberg, Meyer, Marx, Gassl, Hofmann, Ach, Beyschlag, Prey, *Jastaführer* Rudolf Stark, Rudolf Hess (yes, *that* Rudolf Hess), Kranz, Stoer, Ludovici and Hauft, the non-flying OzbV *(A Imrie via HAC/UTD)*

APPENDICES

All scale drawings are of a Fokker D VII,
and are to 1/32nd scale

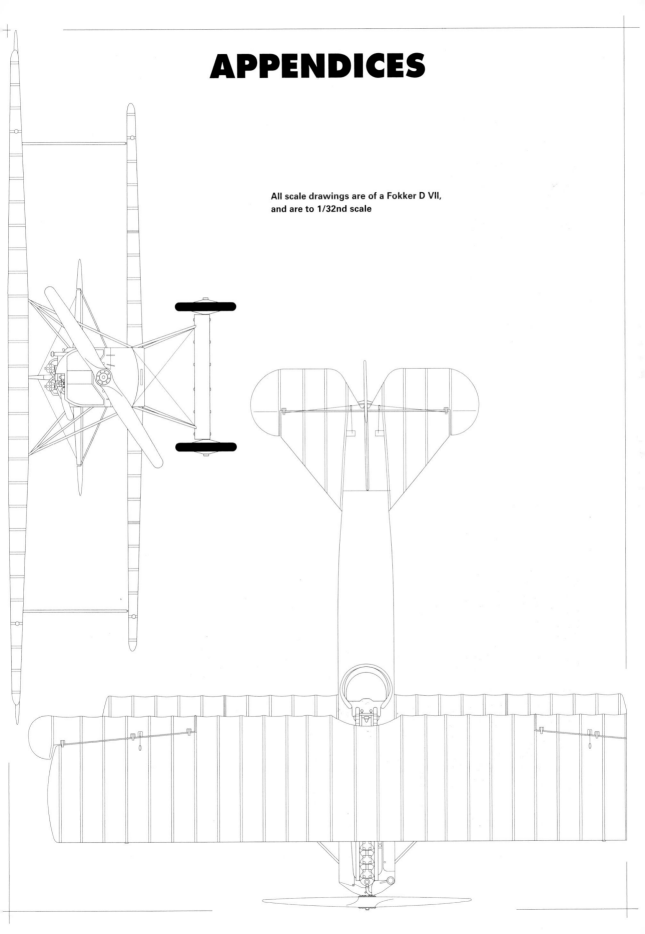

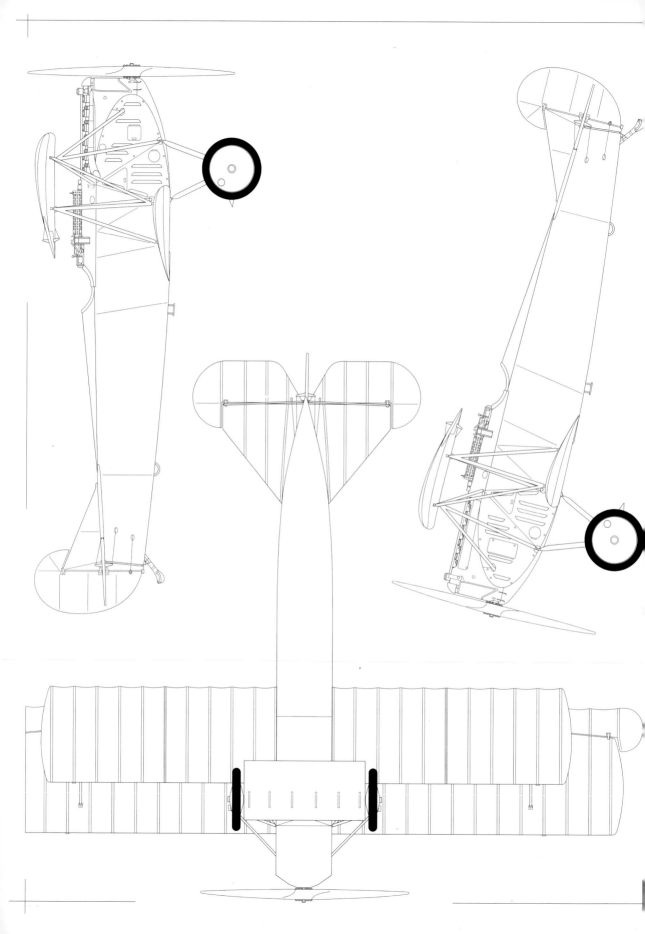

All the artwork in this section has been specially created for this volume by Harry Dempsey, who worked carefully with the authors to illustrate the aircraft as accurately as possible, taking into account the limited information available. Given the myriad variations possible in cowling panel styles, printed fabric applications and other hallmarks of the three D VII manufacturers, it is recognised that these illustrations – many of which are provisional – are far from the last word on this controversial subject. Colours portrayed are approximations at best. The research of Alex Imrie was of particular value, as well as the work of Dan-San Abbot, Dave Roberts and Ray Rimell.

1
Fokker D VII 234/18 of Ltn 'Fritz' Friedrichs, *Jasta* 10, Cappy, circa May 1918

One of the very first production aircraft, this machine was wrecked by 'Fritz' Friedrichs when he collided with two parked Fokkers and some tents. Its fuselage and tail were finished in typical olive-brown streaked finish, while four-colour lozenge fabric covered the wings. The factory-applied iron cross insignia on the fuselage and rudder had been altered to a 'thick' *Balkenkreuz* form by using the widest portion of the cross arms as the bar width. The iron cross insignia on the less-accessible wings had the mandated five-centimetre white border, and these had not been changed at the time of the accident. This machine seems to have had a thin white vertical band just ahead of the fuselage cross as a personal marking. The unit's famous yellow nose marking is provisionally depicted as having been applied, but this is not confirmed.

2
Fokker D VII 244/18 of Ltn Aloys Heldmann, *Jasta* 10, Beugneux, June 1918

This familiar D VII was Heldmann's regular aircraft in June, but the classic photos of it show it being borrowed by Lothar von Richthofen of *Jasta* 11. It also bore the Fokker streaked camouflage on the fuselage and four-colour fabric wings, with *Jasta* 10 yellow on the nose. However, this colour had not been applied to the 'N' struts or wheels. The starboard wheel cover was white and the port cover was absent. Fuselage and tail insignia were converted from iron crosses in the same method as 234/18, producing the thick style of cross, albeit with the correct white borders on the length of the cross bars only. Heldmann's personal emblem was the black and white chequered horizontal tail surfaces. What has previously been interpreted as a yellow 'AH' marking on the upper wing by many (including the authors) is probably nothing more than some repair patching – as depicted in the top wing view on page 43 – which nonetheless resembles a monogram emblem in some respects. Heldmann later flew BMW-engined D VII (F) 4264/18, described as having blue squares on the elevators and a blue fuselage.

3
Fokker D VII (serial unknown) of Ltn 'Fritz' Friedrichs, *Jasta* 10, Beugneux, circa early June 1918

This D VII presents some enigmatic problems in its personal markings. It bore a typical early Fokker finish like the preceding two aircraft, and displayed the unit's yellow nose, struts and wheels covers. There was a band of unknown colour (here shown as blue, which is only one possibility) ahead of the fuselage cross. The most puzzling aspect is the heraldic shield emblem just aft of the cockpit. Heldmann recalled that Friedrichs used the colours of Schleswig-Holstein on his aircraft, but this emblem does not seem to derive from any such heraldry. There was clearly a half of a double-headed heraldic eagle on the white segment of the shield, but whatever emblem appeared on the remaining dark half remains indeterminate. It is *very* provisionally depicted as a red field bearing the rest of the eagle, but this is entirely arbitrary and subject to revision.

4
Fokker D VII (serial unknown) of Offz-Stv Paul Aue, *Jasta* 10, Beugneux, June 1918

Aue decorated his Fokker-built D VII with the Saxon coat of arms, outlined in white. This early Fokker product also bore a streaked-finish fuselage and (probably) four-colour 'lozenge' fabric wings. The cross form on the fuselage is similar to that on Friedrichs' preceding machine, and the insignia on the wings probably followed suit. *Jasta* 10 yellow was displayed on the nose, struts and undercarriage.

5
Fokker D VII (serial unknown) of Ltn Arthur Laumann, *Jasta* 10, Bernes, circa August 1918

Laumann, the last *Jasta* 10 commander, flew this later Fokker-built D VII finished entirely in four-colour fabric. It would certainly have borne the usual yellow décor, and Laumann's initials were painted ornately on a fuselage band of unknown colour (here tentatively yellow). The style of engine cowling panels depicted is also very provisional, as these components are not visible in the classic photograph of this aircraft.

6
Fokker D VII (serial unknown) of Oblt Erich Löwenhardt, *Jasta* 10, Puisieux Ferme, August 1918

Löwenhardt's 'bright yellow' D VII is described in several contemporary accounts, but only one distant in-flight photo has ever been seen by the authors. In actuality, the *Jasta* 10 leader probably flew several D VIIs, and this is an entirely provisional reconstruction of his final aircraft – most likely a BMW-powered Fokker product. When interviewed by Alex Imrie, Löwenhardt's mechanic Otto Timm recalled that the 'all yellow' Fokker actually retained its lozenge fabric wings, but that the rest of the fuselage, struts and tail surfaces were yellow. Leader's streamers (probably red-white-black) trailed from the ends of both lower wings.

7
Fokker D VII 286/18 of Ltn Willy Gabriel, *Jasta* 11, Beugneux, June 1918

Thanks to the description and numerous photos Gabriel gave

to Alex Imrie, this classic aircraft is well-documented. Factory-finished in streaky camouflage fuselage and five-colour fabric on the wings, it eventually displayed the famous *Jagdstaffel* 11 red on its engine cowlings, struts and wheels. Gabriel's personal marking was the orange and sky blue striped tail and rear fuselage. Eventually this was augmented by orange stripes applied to the fuselage sides and upper decking.

8

Fokker D VII (F) 294/18 of Oblt Hermann Göring, *Jagdgeschwader* I, Beugneux, July 1918

This is another reconstructed illustration, based entirely on the description in Göring's combat report for 18 July – 'red forward fuselage with yellow tail'. *Jasta* 11 red was no doubt marked on the nose, struts and wheel covers, and the red nose display may in fact have been more extensive than that shown in this profile. The yellow tail was a personal marking, perhaps that of some unknown pilot from whom Göring borrowed this machine. The rest of the aircraft was probably finished very similarly to Gabriel's 286/18.

9

Fokker D VII (serial unknown) of Ltn d R Erich Just, *Jasta* 11, Beugneux, Summer 1918

Six-victory pilot Erich Just emblazoned his D VII with a black and white fuselage sash. Just's D VII most likely bore the *Staffel* red colour in the usual style, and was apparently finished in lozenge fabric – four-colour is depicted.

10

Fokker D VII (F) 4253/18 of Oblt Hermann Göring, *Jagdgeschwader* I, Metz-Frescaty, October 1918

Previously flown by Udet, this aircraft was apparently briefly taken over by Göring after the former's final two victories on 26 September. Göring retained some of the red décor, but had the rear fuselage repainted in his personal white colour. The wings were covered with four-colour fabric. As on his later D VII, the cockpit edge on the port side of this machine was cut down and a handle fixed to the fuselage. A tubular gunsight was also fitted. The works number 2954 appeared at the base of the rudder.

11

Fokker D VII (F) 5125/18 of Oblt Hermann Göring, *Jagdgeschwader* I, Marville, October 1918

Göring's final D VII is well-known from two classic publicity photos, but the extent of any combat flying he actually did in it, if any, remains debatable. The immaculate finish and carefully applied stenciling indicates that this BMW-powered machine was given its white finish at the Fokker factory especially for the JG I *Kommandeur*. A rack for flare cartridges and a flare pistol tube appeared on the starboard side of the cockpit, and the port side again had Göring's typical cut-down cockpit rim and handle.

12

Fokker D VII (serial unknown) of Ltn d R Egon Koepsch, *Jasta* 4, Metz-Frescaty, August 1918

The black nose, struts and wheels of *Jasta* 4 are seen on this Fokker-built machine flown by Koepsch. The BMW-engined aircraft also bore the black and white fuselage borders seen on many (but not all) D VIIs of this *Staffel*, although this black/white décor was thinly applied and somewhat translucent. Four-colour fabric covered the rest of this machine.

13

Fokker D VII (OAW) (serial unknown) of Ltn d R Ernst Udet, *Jasta* 4, Beugneux, June 1918

This aircraft is certainly one of the most famous of the war, yet conversely remains one of the most controversial and enigmatic The only clear, proven image is a retouched halftone printed in *Mein Fliegerleben,* wherein Udet himself obscures much of the airframe. This depiction is something of a compromise between the various theories concerning the actual colours of this short-lived machine. In fact, there is no contemporary documentation available to support the use of red on this D VII. The wing stripes are traditionally shown as red and white, but are here black and white, as they may have been inspired by Udet's earlier experiences with Kirschstein's similarly striped Dr I and also – perhaps – the tail markings of his old command, *Jasta* 37. The nose, struts and wheels are shown as typical *Jasta* 4 black, and his famous legend *Du doch nicht!!* was painted in white letters on the elevators. The machine also displayed a white chevron on the tail, a marking Udet had used on a previous Albatros D V and his Dr I 593/17. At some point in the summer of 1918 Udet began decorating his machines in red as an aid to confirmation of victories – the question is, just when did he start? The fuselage and tailplane are shown as red, but they could just as well have been black. In fact, this aircraft may have looked much like the next D VII. Lastly, it is shown as an early OAW D VII, but it might have been Fokker-built – or there might have been *two* D VIIs with striped wings, judging from one other very poor photograph.

14

Fokker D VII (OAW) (serial unknown) of Ltn d R Ernst Udet, *Jasta* 4, Bernes, August 1918

This D VII is far better documented, but perhaps less attractive, than the famous striped wing aircraft. It was covered in four-colour fabric and bore *Jasta* 4's black colour on the usual components, along with the black/white fuselage trim often seen in this unit. It also featured Udet's favoured *LO!* insignia and white chevron on the tailplane and elevators. Leader's streamers were also affixed to each elevator.

15

Fokker D VII (F) 4253/18 of Oblt d R Ernst Udet, *Jasta* 4, Escaufort by Busigny, September 1918

Udet's combat reports for 8 August and for his last victories on 26 September describe 4253/18 as having a red fuselage with *'LO!'* insignia and leader's pennants attached to the elevators. This BMW-engined aircraft apparently previously served in *Jasta* 11, and may well have retained its red nose, wheels and struts as illustrated. The witness reports which accompanied Udet's final victory attest to the high visibility of this 'bright red' aircraft with its four-colour fabric-covered wings.

16

Fokker D VII (serial unknown) of Ltn d R Richard Wenzl, *Jasta* 6, Beugneux, June 1918

This early Fokker-built aircraft in streaked finish may have been Wenzl's first D VII. It displayed the standard *Staffel* markings of zebra-striped tailplane/elevators, nose and wheel covers. Wenzl applied his traditional personal black/white fuselage band in the proportions of the Iron Cross ribbon, but with colours reversed. Additional louvres were crudely hacked out of the upper cowling panels in an attempt to improve engine cooling. The wings are shown in four-colour fabric, but five-colour is also possible.

17

Fokker D VII (OAW) (serial unknown) of Ltn d R Ulrich Neckel, *Jasta* 6, Busigny, September 1918

Thought to be Neckel's first *Jagdstaffel* 6 Fokker, this machine had the black/white nose stripes extended the entire length of the fuselage. The standard *Jasta* 6 unit markings appeared on the tail and wheel covers, with four-colour fabric on the wings. Previously, the authors thought the fuselage stripes went across the fuselage decking at an oblique angle, but it now seems more likely they were perpendicular to the centre line as shown.

18

Fokker D VII (serial unknown) of Hptm Rudolf Berthold, *Jagdgeschwader* II, Le Mesnil, June 1918

Berthold's famous Fokker boasted his classic winged sword insignia and the red and dark blue colours of *Jasta* 15, based on his old infantry regiment's tunic. When photographed, this machine displayed red on the wheel covers, struts and engine cowlings, but the fuselage aft to the middle of the cockpit remained in early Fokker-style streaked camouflage. The rest was dark blue. The uppersurfaces of both wings also appear to have been blue, with the exception of an unexplained white panel on the top wing centre section. In his 1930s writings, *Jasta* 15 member von Ziegesar claimed that all of the unit's Fokkers had blue wings, but photographic evidence does not bear this out.

19

Fokker D VII (serial unknown) of Ltn d R Josef Veltjens, *Jasta* 15, Chéry-les-Pouilly, August 1918

Veltjens had his aircraft decorated with the usual red and blue colours and two white stripes on the horizontal tail surfaces to denote the *Staffel* commander. His traditional personal emblem was the so-called 'Indian arrow' in white, which had also decorated all of his previous Albatros fighters. The struts were probably painted light grey, with factory finish wheel covers.

20

Fokker D VII (serial uknown) of Ltn Oliver von Beaulieu-Marconnay, *Jasta* 15, Chéry-les-Pouilly, August 1918

It is believed this was one of Berthold's former machines, as his winged sword insignia can just be made out beneath the dark blue. It was an early Fokker-built D VII which bore the standard *Jasta* 15 colours and the pilot's *4D* insignia based on the branding iron emblem of his former regiment (the 4th Dragoons). This D VII had apparently been fitted with a BMW engine, an unusual windscreen and heavily altered cowling panels with additional louvres. This being one of Berthold's former mounts, its wings were seemingly overpainted blue

on their uppersurfaces as well. A pale-coloured area on the starboard top wing is not explained.

21

Fokker D VII (serial unknown) of Ltn d R Hugo Schäfer, *Jasta* 15, Carignan, November 1918

Schäfer's D VII was also Fokker-built, and featured the usual *staffel* coloration. His personal emblem was a fanciful winged serpent, with a slightly different version applied to the upper fuselage decking. The struts were probably grey, with standard factory-finish wheel covers. The wings were apparently covered with five-colour fabric.

22

Fokker D VII 382/18 of Ltn Georg von Hantelmann, *Jasta* 15, Le Mesnil, June 1918

Hantelmann's D VII was being flown by new *Jasta* 15 member Ltn Kurt Wüsthoff when he was shot down and captured on 17 June 1918, and thus it became the subject of close scrutiny by the Allies. An early Fokker-built D VII, it left the factory with five-colour fabric on its wings and a streaked fuselage. At *Staffel* 15 it was given a red nose and wheels and a dark blue fuselage and tail, but the struts remained grey. The fuselage cross was still slightly visible beneath the blue paint. Hantelmann's skull and crossbones emblem was inspired by his former service as a 'death's head' hussar.

23

Fokker D VII (serial unknown) of Vzfw Gustav Klaudat, *Jasta* 15, Chéry-les-Pouilly, August 1918

Like others in his unit, Klaudat chose to symbolise his former cavalry service with his personal marking, the Uhlan lance with black and white pennant. Otherwise, this Fokker-built machine bore a finish similar to other *Jasta* 15 D VIIs. This profile is based on a rather poor photo, and aspects of it remain provisional.

24

Fokker D VII (serial unknown) of Ltn d R Alfred Greven, *Jasta* 12, Carignan, October 1918

Alfred Greven, a four-victory pilot, previously flew an early OAW-built D VII and also a Siemens-Schuckert D III with *Jasta* 12, both of which bore his white lightning bolt personal emblem. This BMW-engined D VII was turned over to the Americans after the war. It displayed the *staffel* colours of dark blue fuselage and white nose, and probably four-colour fabric on the wings.

25

Fokker D VII (OAW) (serial unknown) of Ltn Franz Büchner, *Jasta* 13, Trier, November 1918

This was the last of at least three different D VIIs flown by Büchner during his time as CO of *Jasta* 13. As such, it bore the final version of the *staffel* colours, with dark green cowling panels bordered by a thin white stripe and the blue fuselage. Büchner's bold personal markings consisted of a leonine 'werewolf's head' on a green panel, and a chequerboard band in the green and white colours of Saxony. The wings were covered in four-colour fabric on both upper and lower surfaces, with pale rib tapes. A tube for a flare pistol exited the fuselage by the cockpit, and additional sights were fitted.

26

Fokker D VII (serial unknown) of Ltn d R Werner Niethammer, *Jasta* 13, Le Mesnil, June 1918

Niethammer's early production Fokker exemplifies the early form of *Jasta* 13 markings, with a dark green nose forward of a demarcation line roughly adjacent to the ammunition chutes and dark blue fuselage/tail. The fin and rudder bore a cross of unusual proportions. The white hammer insignia was an obvious play on words, as 'Niethammer' means 'riveting hammer'.

27

Fokker D VII (OAW) (serial unknown) of Ltn d R Werner Niethammer, *Jasta* 13, Carignan, November 1918

This later OAW-built D VII bore the pilot's white hammer on both the fuselage sides and top, and the later form of *Jagdstaffel* marking. The wings were covered in four-colour fabric, with light rib tapes.

28

Fokker D VII (serial unknown) of Vzfw Albert Haussmann, *Jasta* 13, Le Mesnil, June 1918

Haussmann's Fokker-built D VII came to grief after a mid-air collision that resulted in a forced landing and minor head injuries for the pilot. This aircraft displayed the initial form of *Staffel* green and blue markings, and Haussmann's personal two-colour 'engrailed' band. This band is provisionally illustrated as red and black, which is purely speculative. The wheel covers and cabane struts are also tentatively shown as being green in colour.

29

Fokker D VII (F) (serial unknown) of Oblt Karl Bolle, *Jasta* Boelcke, Aniche, November 1918

Staffelführer Bolle decorated his BMW-engined D VII with his traditional fuselage bands in yellow (the colour of his old cavalry regiment) and Prussian black and white. The remainder of the fuselage was also black, excepting the *Jasta* markings of a white nose and black/white tail. Two white stripes on the four-colour fabric upper wing helped distinguish the *Jasta* commander's machine.

30

Fokker D VII (OAW) 4453/18 of Ltn Alfred Lindenberger, *Jasta* Boelcke, Aniche, November 1918

Lindenberger's OAW-built D VII had its fuselage apparently decorated in two-colour stripes, although this finish was very worn when photographed after the war in Nivelles, Belgium. The colours of these stripes are unconfirmed, but black and yellow is shown, based on the colours of Württemberg's Gold Military Merit Medal. This machine also boasted the *Jasta* Boelcke markings of a black/white tail and a white nose, and had four-colour fabric on the wings.

31

Fokker D VII (F) (serial unknown) of Ltn d R Otto Löffler, *Jasta* Boelcke, Aniche, November 1918

According to the late A E Ferko, this BMW-engined Fokker of *Jagdstaffel* Boelcke may have been flown by ten-victory ace Löffler, and it is thus tentatively attributed. It displayed a black zig-zag stripe on a white band, four-colour fabric and standard

unit markings. The engine cowling aft of the white nose section seems black.

32

Fokker D VII (serial unknown) of Oblt Bruno Loerzer, JG III, Aische-en-Befail, circa November 1918

As befitted a *Geschwader* leader's machine, Loerzer's D VII bore not only the black and white fuselage bands of his old *Jasta* 26, but also had those markings extended to the top of the upper wing and the underside of the lower wing. The unpainted portions of the wings retained their five-colour fabric finish, with rib tapes of the same material. Black/white leader's streamers trailed from the interplane struts. Note that the wing crosses were not full-chord.

33

Fokker D VII (serial unknown) of Oblt Bruno Loerzer or Ltn d R Franz Brandt, *Jasta* 26 and JG III, Aische-en-Befail, November 1918

Looking much like the preceding aircraft, this Fokker-built D VII was photographed in Allied hands after the war in a very war-weary condition. Nonetheless, it still bore the striking *Jasta* 26 black/white décor, including a striped underside on the lower wing. It differs from Loerzer's machine above in that the wing crosses were full chord. The uppersurface of the top wing was apparently also striped, but in colours other than black and white (here provisionally shown as light blue and black?). This aircraft may have also been flown by Loerzer, or perhaps by a deputy leader or the *Jasta* 26 commander Franz Brandt (ten victories).

34

Fokker D VII (F) (serial unknown) of Oblt Theodor Hermann Dahlmann, JG III, Lieu St Amand, September 1918

Theodor Dahlmann served as JG III Adjutant and flew this BMW-engined D VII in *Jasta* 26 colours to bring his score to seven by the end of October. The only known photo of this Fokker shows only Dahlmann's personal emblem of a winged helmet of the valkyries of Nordic mythology. It included the legend *Walküre* and a black frame. Much of the rest of this profile is provisional, but the aircraft probably bore standard *staffel* markings and wings in printed 'lozenge' fabric.

35

Fokker D VII 278/18 of Oblt Hermann Göring, *Jasta* 27, Mont de Soissons Ferme, June 1918

Göring's combat reports for his 19th victory on 5 June 1918 and his 21st victory on the 17th describe the markings of D VII 278/18 as a 'white engine cowling, white tail', and photos of what is probably this machine reveal the struts and wheels were also painted in Göring's personal white colour. This was an early Fokker-built machine which would have had the usual streaky camouflage on the fuselage and five-colour fabric on the wings. The *Jasta* 26 commander achieved his 20th victory on 9 June in 324/18, which was painted similarly.

36

Fokker D VII (OAW) (serial unknown) of Ltn d R Friedrich Noltenius, *Jasta* 27, Chambry, September 1918

Noltenius was flying this OAW-built D VII when he narrowly

survived flying through the debris from a balloon he flamed on 14 September. His individual markings were the stripes on the fuselage and upper wing, in the Hanseatic League colours of red and white. The wings and fuselage were otherwise covered in four-colour fabric which had been somewhat subdued by over-varnishing. The nose does not seem to be yellow as prescribed for *Jasta* 27, but the tailplane is provisionally depicted in the *staffel* colour. The serial number of this machine has been mistakenly reported as Fokker-built 5056/18, but that was actually the D VII flown by Noltenius in *Jasta* 6, which bore similar red/white personal markings.

37
Fokker D VII (Alb) (serial unknown) of Oblt Robert Greim, *Jasta* 34b, Bévillers, September 1918

Greim's Albatros-built D VII featured the *Staffel* marking of a whitish-silver rear fuselage and tailplane, and Greim's traditional personal emblem of two red bands encircling the fuselage. The rest of the machine was probably in four-colour fabric, with factory-finish greyish green cowling panels.

38
Fokker D VII (Alb) (serial unknown) of Vzfw Johann Pütz, *Jasta* 34b, Bévillers, September 1918

Greim's loyal and capable wingman in the summer of 1918 was Johann Pütz, whose D VII was probably very similar to his commander's except for his two green bands. This is confirmed by Rudolf Stark's paintings as well as writings by Stark and Greim. On 23 August 1918, Greim and Pütz joined in attacking British tanks, and Greim would be credited with the destruction of one of them.

39
Fokker D VII (OAW) 4523/18 of Ltn d R Rudolf Stark, *Jasta* 35b, Bühl, October 1918

Stark's well-documented Fokker is seen in its final livery, after several stages of painting. Personal markings were the black-bordered lilac fuselage band, tail and lilac nose. The white *Li* initials were a late addition. Most aircraft in the *staffel* bore a unit marking of a white chevron on the upper wing, but Stark's was lilac, with a black version on the lower wing undersides. Four-colour fabric covered the airframe.

40
Fokker D VII (OAW) (serial unknown) of Hptm Eduard von Schleich, JG IV, Bühl, October 1918

This provisional illustration is based entirely on Stark's descriptions and paintings, as no photos are known to the authors. The 'black knight's' OAW-built D VII of the 4500/18 series featured a black fuselage, undercarriage and (probably) tailplane. The pilot's famous Bavarian lion emblem on a circular field of blue/white diamonds faced forward on both sides of the fuselage. Blue and white streamers were attached to both lower wings at mid-point, and the wings retained their four-colour finish.

INDEX

References to illustrations are shown in **bold**. Plates are shown with page and caption locators in brackets.

aerodromes
  Aniche **77**
  Chéry-les-Pouilly **64**
  Metz-Frescaty **49**
Aue, Offz-Stv Paul **13**, 13-14, **14**, **4**(33, 91)

BMW IIIa engine `23-25, 26
Bähren, Ltn **13**
Bassenge, Gerhard **74**, 77
Bäumer, Ltn Paul **76**, 76-77, **77**
Bavarian *Jagdgeschwader* IV 8, **40**(42, 95), **86**, 86-88
Beane, Lt James D, DSC, CdG 54
Beaulieu-Marconnay, Ltn Oliver 'Beauli' Freiherr von **20**(37, 43, 93),
  64, 64, **65**, 67, **68**, 70
Becker, Ltn Hermann 53-54
Bender, Ltn d R Julius **31**
Berthold, Hptm Rudolf **18**(37, 93), **51**, 51-53, **52**, **62**, 62
Besser, Ltn Hans 54-55
Bodenschatz, Oblt Karl 10, 21, **28**
Boenigk, Oblt Oskar Freiherr von **53**, 53, **55**, **71**
Bolle, Oblt Karl **29**(40, 45, 94), **74**, 74-75
Bormann, Ernst **74**, 77-78
Brandt, Ltn d R Franz **33**(41, 94), 78
Brereton, Maj Louis 62
Bristol F 2B **83**
Brown, 1Lt Ben 49
Büchner, Felix **56**, 61, 62
Büchner, Ltn Franz **25**(39, 93), 55-56, **56**, **57**, 57-59, **58**, **59**, 60, 62
Buder, Vzfw Erich 78
Bülow-Bothkamp, Harry and Walter von 85

Classen, Vzfw Fritz 78-79

Dahlmann, Oblt Theodor Hermann **34**(41, 94), 80, 81
de Havilland DH 4: **4**
Doyle, Capt John E, DFC 29-30
Drekmann, Ltn Heinrich 'Heinz' 27, 31

Everbusch, Alfred 71

Falkenhayn, Oblt Fritz von 8
Fokker, Anthony 7, 16, **73**
Fokker D VII 7, 8, 10, 47
  JG I **18**(37, 93), 64
  JG II **32**(40, 44, 94), **33**(41, 94), **72**
  Jasta 4: **27**, **12**(35, 44, 92)
  Jasta 6: **26**, **16**(36, 46, 92-93), **47**, 49
  Jasta 10: **12**, **13**, **14**, **3**(33, 43, 91), **4**(33, 91), **5**, **6**(34, 91)
    234/18: **6**, 1(33, 91)
    244/18: **17**, **2**(33, 43, 91)
  Jasta 11: **18**, **20**, **9**(35, 92)
    286/18: **20**, **21**, **7**(34, 46, 91-92)
  Jasta 12: **24**(38, 93), **64**
  Jasta 13: **26**, **28**(39, 94), **56**, **60**, **61**, **64**
  Jasta 15: **19**, **20**(37, 43, 93), **21**(38, 43, 93), **23**(38, 93), **51**, **63**,
    64, **66**, **67**, **68**
    382/18: **4**, **22**(38, 93), **65**, **66**, 68-69
  Jasta 26: **33**(41, 94), **72**, **78**, **79**
    501/18: **76**
  Jasta 27: **80**, **83**, **84**
    278/18: **35**(41, 94), **81**
  Jasta Boelcke (2) **74**, **77**
Fokker D VII (Alb) (Albatros-built) 8, **37**(42, 45, 95),
  38(42, 95), **87**
Fokker D VII (F) (BMW-engined)
  JG I
    294/18: **8**(34, 92)
    4253/18: **15**, **16**, **10**(35, 92)
    5125/18: 15, **16**, **11**(35, 92)
  JG III **34**(41, 94)
  Jasta 4: **30**
    4253/18: **15**(36, 92), **28**, 29
  Jasta 10 4264/18: **13**
  Jasta 15: **64**
  Jasta Boelcke (2) **29**(40, 45, 94), **31**(40, 94), **75**
Fokker D VII (OAW) (OAW-built) 8
  JG IV **40**(42, 95)
  Jasta 4: **26**, **13**, **14**(36, 44, 92)
  Jasta 6: **17**(37, 46, 93), **48**
  Jasta 12: **54**, 64
  Jasta 13: **25**(39, 93), **27**(39, 94), **56**, **57**, **58**, **59**
  Jasta 19: **70**
  Jasta 27: **36**(41, 45, 94-95), **82**
  Jasta 35b **88**
    4523/18: **39**(42, 46, 95), **87**, **88**
  Jasta Boelcke (2) 4453/18: **30**(40, 45, 94), **74**, **76**

Fokker Dr I triplane 7, 50, **80**
Fokker Eindecker 7
Fokker V 11 and V 18: 8
Förster, Ltn Otto **18**
Frey, Flieger **74**
Freytag, Ltn d R Alfred **86**
Friedrichs, Ltn Friedrich 'Fritz' **6**, **11**, 11-12, **12**, **1**(33, 91), **3**(33, 43, 91)
Frommherz, Hermann **74**, **81**, 81-82
Fruhner, Vzfw Otto 80-81, 84

Gabriel, Walter 20, 22
Gabriel, Vzfw (later Ltn) Willi **20**, 20-22, **21**, 23, **7**(34, 46, 91-92)
German Air Service 6, 7
  Jagdgeschwader (JG) 9
    JG I Richthofen 8-9, **15**, **16**, **8**(34, 92), **10**, **11**(35, 92)
    JG I commanders 14-15
    JG II 8, **18**(37, 93), 50-51, **51**
    JG II commanders 51-53
    JG III 8, **32**(40, 44, 94), **33**, **34**(41, 94), **72**, 72, 73
    JG IV 8, **40**(42, 95), **86**, 86-88
  Jagdgruppe 9
  Jagdstaffel (*Jasta*)
    Jasta 4: 8, 25-31, **26**, **27**, **28**, **30**, **31**, **12**(35, 44, 92), **13**,
      14(36, 44, 92), **15**(36, 92)
    Jasta 6: 8, **26**, 31-32, **16**(36, 46, 92-93), **17**(37, 46, 93),
      47, 47-49, **48**, **49**
    Jasta 10: **6**, 8-14, **12**, **13**, **14**, **17**, **1**, **4**(33, 91), **2**, **3**(33, 43, 91),
      5, **6**(34, 91)
    Jasta 11: 8, 15-23, **18**, **20**, **21**, **7**(34, 46, 91-92), **9**(35, 92)
    Jasta 12: 8, **24**(38, 93), 53-55, **54**, **55**, **64**
    Jasta 13: 8, **25**(39, 93), **26-28**(39, 94), 55-62, **56**, **57**, **58**,
      59, **60**, **61**, **64**
    Jasta 15: 8, **19**, **20**(37, 43, 93), **21**(38, 43, 93), **22**,
      23(38, 93), **51**, 62-69, **63**, **64**, **65**, **66**, **67**
    Jasta 18 pilots **62**
    Jasta 19: 8, 69-71, **70**
    Jasta 23b 8, 86
    Jasta 26: 8, **33**(41, 94), **72**, **76**, **78**, 78-81, **79**
    Jasta 27: **35**(41, 94), **36**(41, 45, 94-95), **80**, **81**, 81-85,
      82, **83**, **84**
    Jasta 32b 8, 86-87, **88**
    Jasta 34b 8, **37**(42, 45, 95), **38**(42, 95), 86, **87**, 88
    Jasta 35b 8, **39**(42, 46, 95), 86, **87**, 87
    Jasta 35b pilots **88**
    Jasta 36: 8, 85-86
    Jasta Boelcke (2) 8, **29**, **30**(40, 45, 94), **31**(40, 94), 73-78,
      74, **75**, **76**, **77**
  Geschwader-Stock **17**
Gluszewski, Ltn Heinz Graf von **31**
Göring, Oblt Hermann **15**, **16**, **17**, 20-21, 22, **8**(34, 92), **10**, **11**(35, 92),
  71, 72
  on BMW engine 23-24, 25
  with *Jasta* 27: 15, **35**(41, 94), **73**, **80**, **81**, 81
Grassmann, Ltn Justus 12, **13**
Greim, Oblt (later Ritter von) Robert **37**(42, 45, 95), **87**, 87
Greven, Ltn d R Alfred **24**(38, 93), **54**, 54, **64**
Grimm, Ltn d R **56**
Gudenberg, Eberhard von **74**

Hantelmann, Ltn Georg von **4**, **22**(38, 93), 62, 63, 64-66, **65**,
  66, 67, 68
Haussmann, Vzfw Albert **28**(39, 94), **60**, **61**, 61
Hazell, Capt T F, DSO, DFC 28
Heemsoth, Johann **74**
Heldmann, Ltn Aloys 12, **13**, **17**, **2**(33, 43, 91)
Hennig, Uffz **13**
Hess, Rudolf **13**
Hetze, Ltn d R Kurt 61-62, **62**
Hildebrandt, Ltn d R Robert **31**
Hübner, Vzfw Alfred 85, 86
Hutterer, Uffz Michael **88**

Jacobs, Josef **71**
Janzen, Ltn Johann 31
Just, Ltn d R Erich 18, **20**, 20, **9**(35, 92)

Kirschstein, Ltn Hans 32, **73**
Klaiber, Vzfw Otto 54
Klamt, Uffz **13**
Klaudet, Vzfw Gustav **23**(38, 93), **68**, 69
Klein, Hans **71**
Klein, Ltn Johannes 69
Klimke, Ltn Rudolf **84**, 84
Koch, Emil 86-87
Koepsch, Ltn d R Egon 29, **30**, 30, **31**, 31, **12**(35, 44, 92)
Kohlbach, Ltn **13**
Körner, Ltn Hans 70
Kraut, Ltn d R Richard **31**
Krefft, Ltn d R Constantin **73**

Lange, Helmut 80
Laumann, Ltn Arthur 12-13, **13**, **5**(34, 91)
Leusch, Ltn d R Wilhelm 70, **71**, 71

Lindenberger, Ltn Alfred **30**(40, 45, 94), **74**, **75**, **76**, 76
Loerzer, Oblt (later Hptm) Bruno **32**(40, 44, 94), **33**(41, 94),
  71, **72**, 72-73, **73**, 78, 80
Loerzer, Fritz 78
Löffler, Ltn d R Otto **31**(40, 94), **74**, **75**, 75-76
Löwenhardt, Ltn (later Oblt) Erich 9, 10, **11**, 11, **26**, **28**, **6**(34, 91)
Lux, Vzfw Albert 79, 84

Mallinckrodt, Ltn Friedrich **73**
Markgraf, Flieger 32
Matzdorf, Ltn **49**
Maushake, Ltn Heinrich 30-31, **31**
May, Capt W R 84
Mesch, Vzfw Christian 79
Meyer, Ltn Karl **28**
Mynereck, Flieger **74**

Neckel, Ltn d R Ulrich **17**(37, 46, 93), **48**, 49, **56**, 70
Neuenhofen, Wilhelm 85
Niethammer, Ltn d R Werner **26**, **27**(39, 94), **56**, 57-61, **59**, **60**
Nöldecke, Ltn d R Werner **49**
Noltenius, Armin **82**
Noltenius, Ltn d R Friedrich Theodor 23, **36**(41, 45, 94-95),
  48-49, 80, **82**, 82-84, **83**

Operation *Michael* 7, 8, 50

parachute harness, Heinecke **13**, **17**, **31**, **56**, **86**
Pfalz D XII **88**
Pippart, Ltn d L Hans 69-70, **70**
Prey, Gefr **88**
Putnam, Lt David 65
Pütz, Vzfw Johann **38**(42, 95), **87**, 87

Quandt, Theodor 85-86

Reinhard, Hptm Wilhelm 9, 10, 14, 20, 21
Richardson, Lt G **55**
Richthofen, Maj Albrecht von **17**
Richthofen, Lothar von 10-11, 16-19, **17**, **18**, 24-25, **73**
Richthofen, Rittmeister Manfred von 7, 8, 19
Richthofen, Wolfram Ulf von 18, 19
Rienau, Ltn Rudolf 70, 71
Ritter, Ernst de 84
Rohde, Flieger **31**
Royal Air Force No 27 Sqn **4**
Royal Air Force No 70 Sqn 80, 83-84

SPAD XIII **11**
Schaefer, Ltn Friedrich **28**
Schäfer, Ltn d R Hugo **21**(38, 43, 93), **62**, 64, **67**, 69
Scheicher, Ltn Alfons **88**
Schibilsky, Ltn **13**
Schleich, Oblt (later Hptm) Eduard Ritter von **40**(42, 95), **86**, 86
Schliewen, Ltn **49**
Schmidt, Ltn d R Julius **49**
Schubert, Fw Ltn Fritz **73**
Seekatz, Friedrich **73**
Seywald, Ltn Heinrich **86**, 86
Stark, Ltn d R Rudolf **39**(42, 46, 95), **86**, **87**, 87-88, **88**
Steinhäuser, Werner 21
Stoer, Ltn **88**
Suer, Wilhelm **74**
Summers, Capt John K, MC 18, 19, 47

Taplin, Lt L T E, DFC 79
Taylor, Lt R E 27-28
Turck, Oblt Ernst Wilhelm **62**, 62-63
Tutschek, Hptm Adolf von 50

Udet, Ernst 10, 25-29, **26**, **27**, **28**, **29**, **13**, **14**(36, 44, 92),
  15(36, 92), **71**
United States Air Service
  17th Aero Sqn 75
  20th Aero Sqn 54-55
  148th Aero Sqn 19, 75

Vaughn, George A, Jr 85
Veltjens, Ltn d R Joseph 'Seppl' **4**, **19**(37, 43, 93), 53, **62**, **63**, 63-64,
  64, 66, **71**

Walker, Lt Kenneth Mac K 18, 47
Watson, Lt Ken 80
Wedel, Oblt Erich Rudiger von 22-23, **23**
Wense, Ltn Bodo von der 32, 47
Wentz, Ltn Alfred 11
Wenzel, Ltn Paul 32, **47**, 47
Wenzl, Ltn d R Richard 9-10, 11, 15, 22, 23, 32, **16**(36, 46, 92-93),
  47, 47-48
Winterfeld, Ltn Joachim von 30, **31**
Wiser, Lt G B **55**
Wüsthoff, Ltn Kurt **65**, 68-69, 93

Ziegesar, Ltn Joachim von **4**, 66-68, **68**